i P

MW01077692

The Beginners & Seniors Guide to Unlock the Useful,

Time Saving & Fun Features in iPadOS 13.2

The Simplified Manual for Kids and Adults (4th Edition)

Dale Brave

ISBN: 978-1-63750-233-4

Table of Contents

Introduction

An iPad can be so many things: an entertainment hub, a way to stay in touch with the world, a productivity tool, and many other things.

In this friendly, easy-to-follow guide, you'll find out how to fire up any model of iPad, connect to the internet, and use applications to play games, watch movies, listen to music, chat via video, update your social accounts, read the news, or just about anything else you'd want to do.

This book is a perfect guide for all of model of iPad Tablets such as iPad 2, iPad 6th generation, iPad 7th generation), iPad 4th generation, iPad Air, iPad Air 2, iPad Pro 12.9-inch, iPad Pro 9.7-inch, iPad Pro 10.5-inch, iPad Pro 11-inch, iPad Air 3rd generation, iPad mini and many more model to be made with exclusive features.

This book is regularly updated, and it includes the basic setup wizard information and several other tips and tricks to maximize your iPad devices.

In this book, you will find Step-by-step instructions including how to fix common iPad Pro 11 and other model problems in simple and clear terms.

The book is easy, clear, readable, and focuses on what you want to do with your iPad such as:

- Screen splitting of your iPad device
- How to extends iPad's battery strength
- Personalizing the feel and look of your iPad
- How to use iCloud to restore and share your photos and other essential data online
- Secret features unravelled in the original manual
- How to activate used iPad Pro 11 and others
- How to fix slow iPad problems yourself

- How to use Siri's voice commands to control your iPad and for other exclusive things you never would have imagined.

- How to fix iPad that won't charge or power ON

- How to troubleshoot common iPad problems

...and many more.

The information presented in this book is targeted at *kids, teens, dummies and seniors* using iPad tablets or E-reader in a more easy to understand steps.

This 4th edition of *"The Simplified Manual for Kids and Adults- by Dale Brave"* book is *suitable for kids, teens, adolescents, and adults* who are either dummies or seniors interested in finding an accessible guide, manual and exclusive information on making the most of their iPad Tablets. You're in good hands!

CHAPTER 1

iPad Pro 11 Set-Up Wizard

There is no need for connecting your brand-new iPad to your personal computer, as long as there is a mobile data connection designed for activation. As you end the set-up wizard, you may navigate back by tapping the back arrow at the top left-hand side of the screen and scroll further to another display by tapping another button at the top right-hand corner.

You can commence by pressing down the power button at the top edge of your brand-new iPad. You may want to keep it pressed down for about two seconds until you notice a vibration, meaning the iPad is booting up.

Once it boots up finally, you can start initial set up by

following the processes below;

- Swipe your finger over the display screen to start the set-up wizard.

- Choose the language of preference - English is usually at the top of the list, so there is no problem finding it. However, if you would like to apply a different language, scroll down to look for your desired language, and tap to select the preferred language.

- Choose your country - United States may be near the top of the list. If otherwise, scroll down the list and select the United States or any of your choice.

- You need to connect your iPad to the internet to start its activation. You can test this via a link with a Wi-Fi network. Locate the name of your available network in the list shown, and then tap on it to select it.

- Enter the Wi-Fi security password (you will generally find this written on your router, which is probably known as the WPA Key, WEP Key, or Password) and select Sign up. A tick indication shows you are connected, and a radio image appears near the top of the screen. The iPad will now start activation with Apple automatically. This may take some time!

- In case your iPad is a 4G version, you will be requested to check for updated internet configurations after inserting a new Sim card. You can test this anytime, so, for the present time, tap **Continue**.

- Location services will help you with mapping, weather applications, and more, giving you specific information centred wholly on what your location is. Select whether to use location service by tapping allow location services.

- You would now be requested to create **Touch ID,** which is Apple's fingerprint identification. **Touch ID** allows you to unlock your iPad with your fingerprint instead of your passcode or security password. To set up Tap Identification, put a finger or your thumb on the home button (but do not press it down!). To by-pass this for the moment, tap *setup Tap Identification later*.

- If you are establishing Touch ID, the tutorial instruction on the screen will walk you through the set-up process. Put your finger on the home button, then remove till the iPad has properly scanned your fingerprint. Whenever your print is wholly scanned, you will notice a screen letting you know that tap recognition is successful. Tap **Continue**.

- You will be requested to enter a passcode to secure your iPad. If you create **Touch ID**, you must use a passcode if in any case your fingerprint isn't acknowledged. Securing your computer data is an excellent idea, and the iPad Pro 11vides you with several options. Tap password option to choose your lock method.

- You can arrange a Custom Alphanumeric Code (that is a security password that uses characters and figures), a Custom Numeric Code (digit mainly useful, however, you can add as many numbers as you want!) or a 4-Digit Numeric Code (a high old college pin!). In case you didn't install or setup **Touch ID** you may even have an option not to add Security password. Tap on your selected Security option.

- I would recommend establishing a 4-digit numeric

code, or Touch ID for security reasons but all optional setup is done likewise. Input your selected Security password using the keyboard.

- Verify your Security password by inputting it again. If the Password does not match, you'll be requested to repeat! If indeed they do match, you'll continue to another display automatically.

At this time of the set-up process, you'll be asked whether you have used an iPad before and probably upgrading it, you can restore all of your applications and information from an iCloud or iTunes backup by deciding on the best option. If this is your first iPad, you will have to get it started as new, yet, in case you are moving from Android to an iPad, you can transfer all your data by deciding and choosing the choice you want.

How to Restore iPad Back-up from iCloud or iTunes

If you want to restore your iPad from an iTunes back-up, you may want to connect to iCloud and have the latest version of iTunes installed on it. If you are ready to begin this process, tap **restore** from iTunes back-up on your iPad and connect it to your personal computer. Instructions about how to bring back your data can be followed on the laptop screen.

In case your old iPad was supported on iCloud, then follow the instructions below to restore your applications & data to your brand-new device:

- Tap *Restore* from iCloud back-up.

- Register with the **Apple ID** and Password that you applied to your old iPad. If you fail to recollect the security password, there's a link that may help you reset it.

- The Terms & Conditions screen will show. Tap the links to learn about specific areas in details. When you are ready to proceed, select **Agree**.

- Your **iPad** will need some moments to create your **Apple ID** and hook up with the **iCloud server**.

- You will notice a summary of available backups to download. The most up-to-date backup will be observed at the very top, with almost every other reserve below it. If you want to restore from a desirable backup, tap the screen for *all backups* to see the available choices.

- Tap on the back-up you want to restore to start installing.

- A progress bar will be shown, providing you with

a demo of the advancement of the download. When the restore is completed, the device will restart.

- You would see a notification telling you that your iPad is updated effectively. Tap *Continue*.

- To complete the iCloud set up on your recently restored iPad, you should re-enter your iCloud (**Apple ID**) password. Enter/review it and then tap *Next*.

- You'll be prompted to upgrade the security information related to your *Apple ID*. Tap on any stage to replace your computer data, or even to bypass this option. If you aren't ready to do this, then tap *Next* button.

- **Apple pay** is Apple's secure payment system that stores encrypted credit or debit cards data on your device and making use of your iPad also with your fingerprint to make safe transaction online and with other apps. Select *Next* to continue.

- To *feature/add a card*, place it on a set surface and place the iPad over it, so the card is put in the camera framework. The credit card info will be scanned automatically, and you will be requested to verify that the details on display correspond with your card. You'll also be asked to enter the *CVV* (safety code) from the personal strip behind the card. If you choose (or the camera cannot recognize your cards), you can enter credit card information by hand by tapping the hyperlink. You could bypass establishing **Apple Pay** by tapping *create later*.

- Another screen discusses *iCloud keychain*, which is Apple's secure approach to sharing your preserved security password and payment information throughout all your Apple devices. You might use *iCloud security code* to validate your brand-new device and import present data, or you might be asked to continue registering your keychain if it's your first Apple device. In case you don't want to share vital data with other devices, you should go to *avoid iCloud keychain* or *don't restore passwords*.

- If you selected to set up your **Apple keychain**, you'll be notified to either use Security password (the same one you'd set up on your iPad) or produce a different code. If you're making use of your iCloud security code, you should put it on your iPad when prompted.

- This will confirm your ID when signing on to an iCloud safety code; a confirmation code will be delivered via SMS. You may want to hyperlink your smartphone text code (if you have never distributed one with Apple already) so that the code may be provided as a text. Then enter this code to your iPad if requested, then select *Next.*

- You'll then be asked to create **Siri**. *Siri* is your own digital personal associate, which might search the internet, send communications, and check out data in your device and a lot more, all without having to flick via specific apps. Choose to create Siri by tapping the choice or start Siri later to skip this task for now.

- To set up and create **SIRI**, you will need to speak several phrases to the iPad to review your conversation patterns and identify your voice.

- Once you say every term, a tick will be observed, showing that it's been known and comprehended. Another phrase may indicate that you should read aloud.

- Once you've completed the five phrases, you will notice a display notifying that Siri has been set up correctly. Tap *Continue*.

- The iPad display alters the color balance to help make the screen show up naturally under distinctive light conditions. You can switch this off in the screen settings after the iPad has completed configuring it. Tap *continue* to continue with the setup.

- Has your iPad been restored? Tap begin to transfer your computer data to your brand-new iPad.

- You'll be prompted to ensure your brand-new iPad has enough power to avoid the device turning off in the process of downloading applications and information. Tap *OK* to verify this recommendation.

- You will notice a notification show up on your apps, to download in the background.

How to Move Data From Android

Apple has made it quite easy to move your data from a Google Android device to your new iPad. Proceed to the iOS app. I'll direct you about how to use the application to move your data!

- Using the iPad, if you are on the applications & data screen of the set-up wizard, tap *move data from Google android*.

- Go to the Play Store on your Google android device and download the app recommended by the set-up wizard. When it is installed, open up the app, select **Continue** and you'll be shown the *Terms & Conditions* to continue.

- On your Android device, tap *Next* to start linking your Devices. On your own iPad, select *Continue*.

- Your iPad will show a 6-digit code which has to be received into the Google android device to set the two phone up.

- Your Google android device will screen all the data that'll be moved. By default, all options are ticked - so if there could be something you don't want to move, tap the related collection to deselect it. If you are prepared to continue, tap *Next* on your Google android device.

- As the change progresses, you will notice the iPad display screen changes, showing you the position of the info transfer and progress report.

- When the transfer is completed, you will notice a confirmation screen on each device. On your Android Device, select *Done* to shut the app. On your iPad, tap *Continue Installing iPad*.

- An **Apple ID** allows you to download apps, supported by your iPad and synchronize data through multiple devices, which makes it an essential account you should have on your iPad! If you have been using an iPad previously, or use iTunes to download music to your laptop, then you should have already become an **Apple ID user**. Register with your username and passwords (when you have lost or forgotten your **Apple ID** or password you will see a link that may help you reset it). If you're not used to iPad, select doesn't have an Apple ID to create one for free.

- The Terms & Conditions for your iPad can be seen. Please go through them (tapping on more to study additional info), so when you are done, tap *Agree*.

- You'll be asked about synchronizing your data

with iCloud. That's to ensure bookmarks, connections and other items of data are supported securely with your other iPad's data. Tap *merge* to permit this or *don't merge* if you'll have a choice to keep your details elsewhere asides iCloud.

- **Apple pay** is Apple's secure payment system that stores encrypted credit or debit cards data on your device and making use of your iPad also with your fingerprint to make safe transaction online and with other apps. Select *Next* to continue.

- To *feature/add a card*, place it on a set surface and place the iPad over it, so the card is put in the camera framework. The credit card info will be scanned automatically, and you will be requested to verify that the details on display correspond with your card. You'll also be asked to enter the *CVV* (safety code) from the personal strip behind the card. If you choose (or the camera cannot recognize your cards), you can enter credit card information by hand by tapping the hyperlink. You could bypass establishing **Apple Pay** by tapping *create later*.

- Another screen discusses *iCloud keychain*, which is Apple's secure approach to sharing your preserved security password and payment information throughout all your Apple devices. You might use *iCloud security code* to validate your brand-new device and import present data, or you might be asked to continue registering your keychain if it's your first Apple device. In case you don't want to share vital data with other devices, you should go to *avoid iCloud keychain* or *don't restore passwords*.

- If you selected to set up your Apple keychain,

you'll be notified to either use Security password (the same one you'd set up on your iPad) or produce a different code. If you're making use of your iCloud security code, you should put it on your iPad when prompted.

- This will confirm your ID when signing on to an iCloud safety code; a confirmation code will be delivered via SMS. You may want to hyperlink your smartphone text code (if you have never distributed one with Apple already) so that the code may be provided as a text. Then enter this code to your iPad if requested, then select *Next.*

- You'll then be asked to create **Siri**. *Siri* is your own digital personal associate, which might search the internet, send communications, and check out data in your device and a lot more, all without having to flick via specific apps. Choose to create

Siri by tapping the choice or start Siri later to skip this task for now.

- To set up and create SIRI, you will need to speak several phrases to the iPad to review your conversation patterns and identify your voice.

- Once you say every term, a tick will be observed, showing that it's been known and comprehended. Another phrase may indicate that you should read aloud.

- Once you've completed the five phrases, you will notice a display notifying that Siri has been set up correctly. Tap *Continue*.

- The iPad display alters the color balance to help make the screen show up naturally under distinctive light conditions. You can switch this off in the screen settings after the iPad has completed configuring it. Tap *continue* to continue with the setup.

- Has your iPad been restored? Tap begin to transfer your computer data to your brand-new iPad.

- You'll be prompted to ensure your brand-new iPad has enough power to avoid the device turning off in the process of downloading applications and information. Tap *OK* to verify this recommendation.

- You will notice a notification show up on your apps, to download in the background.

NB: Setting up as new iPad: Similar method, as described above, applies.

CHAPTER 2

iPad Pro 11 Tips & Tricks

Here are some guidelines to help you love the more exceptional features on your iPad Pro 11.

How to Update the iPad Pro 11 Operating System (iOS Version)

Under normal circumstances, the operating-system of your iPad Pro 11 called **iPadOS** would look for updates itself, and also bring to your notice when the first is available by putting a red badge on the configurations icon. It will not set up itself though; you will do that!

To set up an update to iOS, follow the below steps:

- At the home screen, locate and select on **SETTINGS**.

- Inside the settings menu, Tap **GENERAL**.

- Tap on **COMPUTER SOFTWARE UPDATE**.

If the phone is current, you will see a message on-screen letting you know so. When there is any upgrade available, information for this will be shown on-screen together with a setup prompt as a means to begin the revise. You can likewise consent to new terms & conditions for the working device too!

Your phone may restart several time later during the update process, and also you may not have the ability of utilizing it as it's updating. So; it is best to set up an update on your phone when you understand you're not in all probability to need it within the timeframe the update would maintain progress!

How to Manage Notifications

Notifications are your device's way of letting you know what's occurring in an App. This may be information including a note or Email notification, on every occasion you install an App; it'll have its pre-decided configurations about just how it interacts with you (via notifications); nevertheless, you could easily change them, or forestall notifications from happening at all.

Lock display notifications on the iPad Pro 11 will come in two primary forms, banners and Notifications. Banners Appear near the top of the display screen, and Notifications which shows up at the guts of the lock screen. Probably the most glaring difference when working with your iPad Pro 11 is that banners vanish automatically after a couple of seconds; however, notification alert needs an action brought on (typically only a select) before they disappear.

Your iPad Pro 11 has notification middle; which shows

you all the notifications you have obtained within the last 24 hours, that you haven't already taken action on - If you **OKAY** an alert for example, then it will not show in the notification middle.

iPad Pro 11 Notification Settings

Swipe down from the very best side of the iPad Pro 11 screen, and you will see two headings near the top of the screen notifications.

Follow the below process to gain access to the notification middle;

- "Today" gives you an accurate overview of your programs for your day - the weather, any calendar entries, and almost every other things you've gained access to. You might scroll to the low part and edit the Apps that could show information there.

- "Notifications" shows all information from the previous day that you have previously used. All Apps that generate notifications is seen in this list if you don't choose to exclude them (I will display for you ways to do this below).

- Tapping on any notification upon this list will need you to the little bit of information in the App that produced it - Tapping on the tweets notification, for example, would open up the tweets App which specific tweet.

- To clear notifications from confirmed App, select the x at the right-hand part of its name bar, then Tap **CLEAR**. There isn't any clear all function, lamentably, so you will want to achieve that for each App in the list to vacant the list.

How to Change Notification Preferences

Every App gets the same simple configurations as long as notifications are concerned.

- From the home display, find and select **SETTINGS**.

- In the primary settings menu, Tap **NOTIFICATIONS**.

- At the very top, you might see options showing the order where notifications are shown within the notification center. You can transform this by Tapping on this and choosing almost every other option. Below this, you will notice a summary of every one of the Apps on your iPad Pro 11, and beneath their name, you will see their notification options. To edit a credit card application options, Tap its Name.

- You may locate switches to regulate whether to

allow Notifications if to show on Lock Display or in the Notification Centre and various options. You can additionally select if notifications should show as Banners or Notifications when the iPad Pro 11 is unlocked, or by no means, by Tapping the right choice.

While you're pleased with your configuration for the App, Tapping the blue arrow at the very top left-hand corner will lead you back to the menu, helping you to edit various other App's configurations.

How to Use Two Apps simultaneously with Slide Over & Break up View

Do you want to manage your calendar or any other even while you are checking your Email? No issue, this section will show you how.

Need to research something online by safari without dropping off your gained access to on iBooks or any other? Now it's easy!

Slide Over allows you to quickly use the other App without terminating the first (or departing the display) and **SPLIT UP View** will enable you to use two apps on the display screen simultaneously - forget about needing to interchange laterally!

How to Use Two Apps Side-by-Side with Break up View

Having opened the next App with a slip over as instructed above, switching to a split view can be more comfortable.

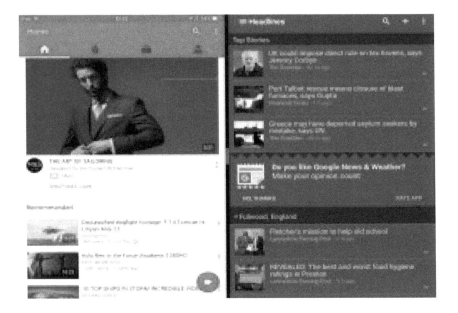

- With another App opened up in slip over, swipe the white pub toward the center of the screen. The dimmed down Background App will brighten again, which indicates that glide over has turned into the split up view. Each App is usable, impartial of each other.

- To improve the other App, swipe the grey pub down from the very best of the screen and select a distinctive App from the list. To close a divided view, pull the divider to the right-hand side of the screen.

As you observe, using split view can be a development of Slip Over, and helps it be easy to "get things achieved" without the difficulty of continually turning back and forth between two Apps. The power of the iPad Pro 11 method is that you will have the capacity of using high-performance Apps side-by-side without it lacking a defeat, that's brilliant if you get a Face Time Video Call if you are in the center of editing an image!

How to Swiftly Use another App with Slide Over

In my instance, I've safari opened up on the screen, and I have to check something on the calendar:

- Together with your first App open up on the screen, SWIPE in from the right-hand advantage of the display to open up **SLIDE OVER**.

- This will open up a panel running the ultimate App you used (previous in the primary windows). To alternative, this to a distinctive or new App, pull down the tiny gray pub from the very best of the Slip Over -panel. The App in the primary windowpane will dim into the background.

- Please scroll through the set of Apps to find the

main one you want to open up and Tap it to open it up in slip over.

- Together with your chosen App opened up, you might now utilize it as if it's been on the original main display screen. To disregard it and go again to your earlier App, swipe the other App to the right-hand corner of the screen.

Notifiction Fast Actions

If you get a text message or email even while you're utilizing your iPad Pro 11, you'll get a banner notification that shows near the top of the screen. You may get off this by swiping it upwards to continue using what you're doing. However, if you swipe it downwards, you'll access three other available choices.

Swiping downwards on the text notification will show the keyboard, letting you instantly answer the message and never have to change application. Swiping down on a contact notification gives you the decision of replying to or deleting the e-mail.

Around the lock display screen, you could additionally swipe from left on a contact notification to send it right to garbage without even unlocking your iPad Pro 11.

Chapter 3

How to Use Drag and Drop Features on an iPad Pro 11

The drag and drop feature involves a multitasking process, and the frequent need to use multiple fingers or both of your hands on the iPad at the same time to move files. Drag and drop is an option to the popularly known *copy-and-paste*; when you move a file from one directory to some other folder on your computer, you are just performing a copy and a paste by making use of your mouse rather than menu instructions; and with the iPad already assisting a standard clipboard, you can duplicate an image from the Photos application to the clipboard, open up the Notes application and paste it into one of your records.

Why do we need Drag and Drop feature?

First, drag-and-drop makes the procedure smoother when you're able to start the Photos application and the Notes application side-by-side and move photos from one to the other. Moreover, you can grab multiple pictures and pull them all simultaneously to the destination folder. This makes it possible to choose multiple images and submit an email reasonably simple.

You can also choose photos from multiple sources, and that means you can grab an image in the Photos app, open up Safari to include an image from a website and then open up your Mail application to drop them into a note.

What to Drag and Drop on an iPad

So, what are the possible items you can pick up?

You can pick up just about anything that may be thought of as an *object*. This consists of pictures, documents, or even chosen text. You can even grab links in the Safari internet browser and drop them into a text, an email, etc. You can also grab a text document from iCloud Drive and drop it into Notepad where it'll show up as the material of the written text file.

Move and drop works both within the same applications and across multiple apps; for instance, you can get a web link in Safari while in scenery setting, move it aside of the display and drop it in to the space that is established to start a break up view of both websites in the web browser, or you move the same hyperlink into a fresh message in the Email app.

How to Drag and Drop on the iPad

The actual notion of drag-and-drop is straightforward,

but its implementation happens to be (and could remain) complex. Dragging an object just like a document or a picture from one place to another is as easy as moving your finger, however when you consider multiple items and multiple apps, you may want to place the iPad on the desk or your lap and use both of the hands.

To get an object, press your finger against the display screen for minutes; the item will pop up from where it is situated in the app, once it pops out of its original place, you can move your finger around the display, and the picture or object will stay trapped to your finger. To get additional purposes, tap them with one of your other fingers; that's where using two hands makes the procedure much more workable. If you're selecting multiple images in the Photos app, you can touch each picture to include these to the items being dragged.

If you are dragging images, website link, text message or

other items, the procedure of the iPad remains exactly like if you weren't dragging anything; this implies that you can close from the application by clicking the *Home Button*, open up another application and drop your selection involved in it.

Moreover, you can start a whole new app and increase your chosen items, but you'll need to employ a new finger to get items from a different app; and, yes, you may use multiple fingertips to drag items, you can as well change fingers; if you will pardon the pun, this is a convenient feature. You can switch the selected item to some other finger on a single hand or even to your other hands; you need to place the 'new' finger near to the finger 'holding' the selected item, and you'll start to see the selection move under the new finger. When the selected item sticks to the new finger, you can lift the initial from the display screen.

As regards the dock for opening applications or multitasking, if you move a finger from underneath the iPad toward the very best, the application dock will be exposed. You should use the dock to open up a new app, or you can pull an application from the dock to the center of the display to open it up together with the application as a floating column; this will help you to use both applications at precisely the same time.

If you know you are dragging in one application and dropping into another app, it is easiest to open up both applications on the display screen first in slide-over or split-view and then move from one application to the other.

How to Use Drag-And-Drop to Transfer images for an iPad

There are a variety of great ways to use the new drag-and-drop feature from selecting photos relating to a document or email message to grabbing selections of text from a website to drop into Notes, but possibly the most versatile is how it can connect to the Files app.

An excellent example is importing photos from your personal computer to your iPad; drag-and-drop can make this a more natural process.

Place your photos within an iCloud folder, open up Documents and Photos in split-view on your iPad, and then use drag-and-drop to move multiple pictures at the same time from the folder in iCloud to whichever album you want to put them into within the Photos app.

There is no need to plug your iPad into your personal computer, use iTunes, or even to transfer from a cloud storage space by conserving each picture to your camera or use a third-party app. In the recent iOS version, it is only a simple drag-and-drop process.

The capability to copy files and photos so easily can be incredibly useful after the Files app facilitates third-party cloud storage services like Dropbox, Google Drive, etc.

CHAPTER 4

How to Fix Common iPad Power Problems

Sometimes whenever your iPad doesn't start, you will think you should buy a new phone. This can be true if the trouble is terrible enough; however, there are diverse methods to be applied on your iPad before you finally conclude that the phone is dead. In case your iPad doesn't **START**, try these six steps to get the problem set yourself.

- **Charge Your Tablet**

Ensure that your iPad's battery is well charged sufficiently to power the smartphone.

If you wish to try this, plug your iPad into a wall structure charger or your personal computer via USB cable, but I strictly recommend using power. Make sure you allow it charge for at least fifteen to thirty minutes. This could make your mobile phone get start up automatically, or you can also press down the power button to carefully turn it ON.

If regardless you think your phone ran out of battery when using or recharging fails, it is feasible that your charger or cable is defective or the battery is terrible which implies you may want to acquire another battery. You can try to use various other cables to check.

- **Restart Your iPad**

If charging the battery didn't Turn your iPad ON or your iPad does not charge while ON and you're sure the charger works on other mobile phones, the next thing you have to try is to restart the phone. This is attained by pressing down the **power button** at the very top right side of the smartphone for a couple of seconds. If the smartphone is OFF, it must turn ON. If it's ON, you will notice the slider offering to turn it OFF.

- **Hard Reset the iPad**

You could attempt a hard reset if the normal restart didn't transform it ON. A hard reset is kind of a restart that clears a higher percentage of the phone's memory space (however not its storage space, you won't lose any document) for a more complete reset.

Follow the below instructions to apply hard reset:

1. Press and hold down the **Power Button** and **Home Button** at the same time. (If you work with the iPad 7 and later versions, Press down **Power** and **Volume Button** at the same time.)

2. Maintain holding down those button for at least ten

seconds (there is certainly nothing at all absurd with holding those button down for 20 or 30 secs, however, if nothing at all has occurred by holding them down, it in all probability won't work)

3. If the Shut-down slider shows up on the screen, maintain pressing the buttons

4. Until when the white Apple logo design appears, after that, you can remove your hands off those buttons and allow phone start up.

5. Restore iPad to Factory Settings.

Sometimes the best strategy is restoring your iPad to its production default settings. This technique will remove all the info and configurations on your phone (You can synchronize and backup your details), and in exchange fix a significant number of problems.

Although typically, you'll synchronize your iPad and restore it using iTunes, however, if your iPad won't activate, try these steps:

1.   Plugin the iPad's **USB cable** to the connection slot, yet not into your personal computer.

2.   Press down the iPad's **Home button** (while on an iPad 7 or later version, press down **Volume button**).

3.   While still pressing down the home button, plug the contrary end of the USB wire into your personal computer.

4.   This will result in opening **iTunes**, it'll automatically place the iPad into recovery setting, and consequently, help you completely restore the iPad.

- **Set iPad in DFU Mode**

In a few situations, your iPad might not get **Started** as it does not boot up. This may happen after jailbreaking the phone or when you try to install an iOS revise without enough space for storage or battery life.

If this is the problem you're facing, you can simply put your mobile phone in **DFU Mode** by following these processes:

1.   Plug your iPad into your personal computer.

2.   Please press down the **Power button** for three mere seconds, then allow it to be.

3.   Press down the **Power button** and the **Home button** (with an iPad 7 or later versions, press **Volume down**) together for approximately 10 seconds.

4.   Release your hands from the **Power button**, however, maintain pressing down the home button (with an iPad 7 or later versions, keep the volume down) for about 5 seconds.

5.   If the screen remains dark and nothing appears noticeable, you're in **DFU Mode**. Adhere to the onscreen instructions in iTunes.

- **Reset Proximity Sensor**

There is undoubtedly another situation that can make your iPad never to turn **ON,** which is a defect in the proximity sensor that dims the iPad's display screen. This causes the screen to remain darkish even if the smartphone is **ON** rather than also near to your face.

Follow the instructions highlighted below;

1.   Press down the home and **Power Button** to restart the phone.

2.   When it restarts, the screen should then be working.

3.   Tap the **Configurations app.**

4.   Tap **General.**

5.   Tap **Reset.**

6.   Tap **Reset All Configurations**. This will erase all your preferences and configurations on the iPad, however, won't delete your data.

If regardless your iPad won't start after these steps; the problem is most likely too severe to revive personally. I would suggest you contact Apple support. The support staff will either repair your phone or let you know what it could cost to fix the problem.

You should check the status of your iPad's warranty before going to the repair center because that could save you additional money on the repair.

CHAPTER 5

How to Connect iPad Pro 11 to your TV Wirelessly and with Cable

The iPad Pro 11 remains a great way to take pleasure in movies and TV, specifically when viewing on that beautiful 12.9-inch iPad Pro 11 Pro. This makes the iPad Pro 11 an unusual way to slice the wire and get rid of cable. Moreover, the newest TV app requires this step further, adding a centralized spot to control all of your loading apps. For everyone who've hunted through each application looking for which channels a specific film or show, we thank Apple!

However, how about watching your TV? If you'd opt for viewing on your large screen, don't get worried, it is on the other hand easy to get your iPad Pro 11 linked to your Television. You can also get it done wirelessly! Plus, you can connect your headphones to any Television to get a non-public watching experience.

Connecting the iPad Pro 11 with a VGA Adapter

Using Apple's VGA adapter, you could hook your iPad Pro 11 up to television outfitted with a VGA input, a pc monitor, a projector, and other display devices that supports VGA. That is amazing for screens. Many modern video screen units aid several display properties; you might even switch between your use of your display screen for your processing device and utilizing it for your iPad Pro 11.

The VGA adapter will also support the screen mirroring mode. However, it generally does not transfer sound, and that means you will either pay attention through the iPad

Pro 11's built-in sound system or exterior speakers founded via the iPad Pro 11's headphone jack.

If you're making programs on viewing through your TV, the HDMI adapter or the component cables will be the best solutions. However, if you intend on utilizing a laptop screen or want to use your iPad Pro 11 for big shows with a projector, the VGA adapter could be an excellent solution.

Do you realize you can view live Television on your iPad Pro 11? There are many add-ons made to help you watch live Television on your iPad Pro 11, access your cable stations and even your DVR from any room inside and while abroad through your computer data connect. Find out ways to watch TV from your iPad Pro 11 as you read further.

Connecting the iPad Pro 11 to your High Definition TV through HDMI Cable

Apple's digital AV adapter is most likely the very best & most straight-ahead way to hook your iPad Pro 11 up to your High definition TV. This adapter lets you connect an HDMI cable from your iPad Pro 11 to your Television. This wire will send the video out to your Television. This means any application that helps video out will arrive in 1080p "HD" quality.

Moreover, preferably Apple TV, the digital AV adapter works with show mirroring, so even applications that do not support video away will screen up to your Television set.

Are you concerned about battery life?

The adapter additionally gives you access for connecting

a USB cable to your iPad Pro 11 that can source power to the unit and keep maintaining that battery from running low when you are binging on Seinfeld or doing other things. You could additionally stream your film collection from your laptop to your iPad Pro 11 via your High definition TV using home posting. This is a long notch process to finally change from DVD and Blu-ray to digital video without dropping the "to view it" on your substantial display TV. You can purchase the apple lightning digital AV adapter on amazon.

Consider: The lightning connector cannot work with the first iPad Pro 11, iPad Pro 11 2 or iPad Pro 11 3. You may want to buy a digital AV adapter with a 30-pin connection for those old iPad Pro 11 models. This makes an Airplay solution like Apple Television even far better for these models.

Connecting the iPad Pro 11 Wirelessly without the utilization of Apple TV via Chromecast

In case you don't have to head the Apple TV path; however nevertheless need for connecting your iPad Pro 11 to your TV without any wires, **Google's Chromecast** can be an alternative solution. It comes with an extraordinarily easy setup process that uses your iPad Pro 11 to configure the Chromecast and get it connected to your Wi-Fi network, and when the whole lot is established and operating, you might connect the iPad Pro 11's screen to your television - as long as the application you are using, works with Chromecast.

Also, that's the best restricting factor when compared with Apple TV: Chromecast support wants to be included in the app when compared with Apple television's

Airplay, which fits with almost every application for the iPad Pro 11.

Why use *Chromecast*? For just one factor, it's much less costly. You could buy a Chromecast for as cheap as $30. It will work with both Google android and iOS devices; if you come with an android phone with your iPad Pro 11, you might use chromecast with all of them. Moreover, with android, chromecast has a function much like Apple TV's screen mirroring.

Connecting an iPad Pro 11 through Composite/Component Cables

In case your TV does not support HDMI, or if you're genuinely working low on HDMI outputs on your HDTV, you can also choose to connect the iPad Pro 11 for your TV with composite or component cables. The amalgamated adapters break up the video to red, blue and green that provides a somewhat better picture, but amalgamated adapters are best designed for the old 30-pin adapters. Component adapters use the one 'yellowish' video wire well suited with the red and white audio cables, that's appropriate for almost all television sets.

The component and composite cables won't support the display mirroring mode on the iPad Pro 11, so they could only use applications like Netflix and YouTube that support video out. Additionally, they flunk of 720p video; therefore, the high-quality will never be as the digital AV adapter or Apple Television.

Unfortunately, these accessories might not be accessible to the more recent lightning connector, so; you'll need a lightning to 30-pin adapter.

Connecting the iPad Pro 11 to your TV with Apple TV and Airplay

Apple TV is an excellent way of connecting your iPad Pro 11 to your Television. While it is expensive over other alternatives, it's the most reliable solution that is mobile. This implies you will keep your iPad Pro 11 on your lap and utilize it as a remote control while sending the screen to your Television. This is the best and quality solution for video games, where using a cord to hook up your iPad Pro 11 on your Television may be prescribing or restricting.

Apple TV uses Airplay to have a connection/interaction with your iPad Pro 11. Most loading apps use airplay and send full-display screen 1080p video to it. However, even applications that don't support Airplay or video out will continue to work via screen mirroring, which replicates your iPad Pro 11's screen on your Television.

Various other bonus of Apple TV is the applications already installed on these devices. If you love *Netflix, Hulu plus* and *crackle*, you certainly do not need to add your iPad Pro 11 to see loading video from these services. The applications run natively on Apple TV. **Apple TV** additionally works amazingly with the iPad Pro 11 and iPod, letting you stream video through Airplay or use your entertainment device's audio speakers to try out music.

Apple currently arrived with a fresh release of Apple TV that works at the same processor used for the iPad Pro 11 air. This helps it be lightning swift. It additionally helps a complete-blown version of the application store, which provides usage of even extra apps. Regrettably, the access-level charge is $149 as at the time of research. The freshest information is the classic (old) Apple TV still works just superb, allowing you to connect your iPad Pro 11 on your TV's display and is currently designed for around $69 as at the time of research.

CHAPTER 6

How to Use App Store Effectively

Do you want to download apps to your iPad? With such a lot to choose from in the app store, it's hard to realize where to begin! Right here's the way to get the tasty morsels of application from the Apple application store for your iPad.

How to Download New App on iPad

Downloading new applications via the app store is a reasonably direct process; however, when you download your first app, you can have a bit of set up to do in regards to your **Apple ID**. Comply with the instructions underneath, and you will have your iPad ever downloading apps right away!

- To begin, tap the App Store icon at the home

screen of your new iPad.

- The store will open up with the Featured Apps web page. This may display to you the applications presently being promoted, either by Apple themselves or via the App developers. You can scroll down the page to look at distinct sections, and each areas' icons can be swiped through to examine which apps are being featured.

- Tapping **See All** at the right-hand side of every featured segment will show you that option in more detail.

- At the top left of the first website, you could select on **Categories**, which breaks up the App Store into broadly titled segments, without difficulty navigating through the sections. Tap **Cancel** at the top to return to the presented apps web page.

- In the categories, you may see sub-categories to

make it simpler to browse the kind of apps you're looking for.

- At the bottom of the leading web page, you'll find links to various sections of the App Store. Featured you will see, and top Charts which are self-explanatory - brief access to **"Top 40 applications"** style lists of free and paid applications if you want to scroll through.

Explore allows you to look for what human nearby are downloading, which can be quite useful when trying to find your way around a new location, or in case you're at a sporting or musical occasion.

Tapping **SEARCH** at the lower part of the display screen allows you to enter the name of an App you have heard about or recommended to you.

Updates, as the name implies, is where you can control your apps and download updates.

- When using the search function, anything you type into the field causes results to auto-fill on the web page. Tap the Search suggestion you like, to see what apps it brings up.

- If the button to the right-hand side of the app's name says **Download**, the app is free, and there will be no price to yourself. Tapping the word **Download** will change the box to say **Install**.

- Tapping Install will start the download process. If

there is a fee, the price would be displayed in place of the term **Download**, and you'll be asked to link a card to your **Apple ID** to pay for this and any future purchases.

- If that is the first app you have attempted to download on your new iPad, you may be requested to input your **Apple ID** information. If you have already got an **Apple ID** (if this is your first iPad you will be prompted to create one at some stage in the initial set up process), you can tap use existing **Apple ID**, and **Sign in**. In case you do not have an Apple ID, select create a new Apple ID and observe the on-screen instructions to create your free Apple ID account. When you have already introduced your Apple ID by signing into iCloud, you will need to put in your password.

- For ease of use, you may set a time hold of 15 or

more minutes before your password is needed again. This can make it smooth to install several apps in one session as you may not need to enter your password every time. Tap to regularly require your security password or require after 15 minutes, as you deem fit to you.

- You'll necessarily need to accept the iTunes Terms & Conditions, and the Apple privacy policy (which you can get dispatched to yourself via email by tapping the supplied hyperlink) by tapping **Agree**, then show that you genuinely do agree by tapping **Agree** again!

- With your account signed in and the agreements handled, your app can now be downloaded. Tap ok for this to happen.

- When the application is downloading, you'll see a blue development indicator in the shape of a circle, with a square at the middle. Tap this if you want to pause/restart the download for any cause.

- When the application has been successfully installed, the progress button changes to an open button to which will let you access the app. When installing, the app will also appear in the first available home display area. However, you can without difficulty move this in case you want!

While you've completed your task in the store, press the **Home button** at the bottom of the iPad's front panel to return to your home display screen. Swipe across to see your newly installed apps!

How to Manage Applications on iPad
How to re-arrange iPad Apps

Whenever you download a brand-new app, it is automatically going to primarily occupy the next available space on your home display. You can easily re-arrange the applications into any order you want. To try this, tap and hold your finger on the application icon for some seconds. All the icons start jiggling. Now, all you want to do is place your finger on the image you need to move and drag it to the precise position of your choice. You can walk in between the display screen by moving the icon at the edge of the screen for a 2nd or 3rd. When you have finished, press the home button to go back to the standard display.

How to Organize iPad Folders

Setting your apps in folders makes it loads quickly to search out the app you're searching. In preference to scrolling through pages of apps, you could click on the appropriate folder and go immediately to the app you want.

To create a folder, all you need to do is place your finger on an app icon until it starts to jiggle similarly to when you are re-arranging apps. Then pull and drop an application icon at the top of another app icon. This will place both applications in a folder. You may change the name of the folder and move in a few more apps if you need. If you have completed the process, press the home button.

To move objects out of a folder, open up the folder first

then maintain your finger on one of the application icons in it until they jiggle, then tap and hold on your selected app, and drag it out of the folder to the home screen. If you pull the remaining last app out of the folder, the folder itself will vanish.

How to Delete iPad Apps

When you have downloaded an application which you do not like or that you don't need again, you may delete it off your iPad. To do that, just press and keep your finger on the app icon till the icons begin jiggling about. You ought to then see an **X** at the top left corner of every icon.

Tap the **"X"** to dispose of the app. Do not worry; you cannot take away inbuilt apps on phone or contacts by doing this so that it won't cause any problem.

Chapter 7

How to Locate Saved Files on an iPad

Your iPad is like having a slim-line PC with you all the time; it could store all of your favourite applications and files, which makes it easier to access essential documents wherever you are in the world. You should understand and know where to find downloads on your iPad and how to control your documents.

Where Are Downloads on My iPad?

Locating where the download is on your iPad is quite easy when you are using iOS on any Apple device, but that isn't the case as it pertains to managing data files. There is no iPad downloads folder where all documents immediately go to like on Personal computer or Mac, and the iOS document system isn't as effortless to search like a Google android file system.

In which a file downloaded is reliant on the app you utilise to see it with, although things have grown to be just a little simpler to understand because of the introduction of the Files application in iOS 11.

Choosing where you can Save a File

It is critical to save your data files to a spot where you can find it again. However, there are various alternatives for saving documents, but here's how to save lots of documents easily from popular apps.

Open up the relevant email: Faucet Options in the very best right of the display, highlighting your options dialogue box

Choose which application to send the document to With regards to the document, you can usually faucet Save Image for images, duplicate to iBooks for PDFs or Save to Documents to save lots of it to the Data files application for general use. The iPad Email app shows email and attachment, highlighting the Save to Documents option. *Tap the greater icon to find more options.*

If you tap Save to Files, after that you can choose to either save the document to your iCloud Drive or right to the iPad, then tap Add; iPad Email App displaying where you can save a connection to if you wish to access the document from other iOS or Mac devices, touch iCloud Drive. Done well, you've successfully preserved the document to your selected location!

Saving a Document from Safari

Here's how to save lots of a document from the default browser, Safari.

- *Open the document in Safari*

- *Tap Options:* iPad Safari application showing where the Options dialogue is on the browser

Choose where you can save it: The Safari browser running with an iPad, with the Save to Data files dialogue box highlighted

You may want to scroll to find more options such as *Save to Files*, depending on how many apps can be found to use the file.

Saving a graphic From Safari

Open up the image in Safari: Keep your finger to the image, then release after an instant or two to talk about the dialogue package.

Touch Save Image to save lots of the image to your Photos folder: A graphic within Safari on the iPad, with Save Image highlighted.

Where to find Downloads on your iPad

Once you have downloaded a file, where do you think it is? Here are the many places your file might be:

Images: if it's an image file, it's probably stored inside your Photos Gallery.

PDF: saving your "file to iBooks," PDF documents are sent or copied to iBooks.

Other Documents: For all the data files, it's probably stored in the Data files App. This application brings together all of your documents across iCloud so that it can likewise incorporate documents from your Mac or other iOS devices.

Chapter 8

How to Create a Folder on an iPad

We've all been there (searching through web page after web page of application icons looking for where we put our Facebook application or that favorite game we haven't used in some time). The best thing about the iPad is just how many amazing applications you can download, but this includes a price: a great deal of applications on your iPad! Fortunately, there's one great technique for maintaining your iPad structure (you can make a folder for your apps).

Developing a folder on the iPad is one particular task that truly is as easy as 1-2-3.

- *Grab the application with your finger*: If you aren't acquainted with moving apps around the iPad display, you can "grab" an application by keeping your finger onto it for a couple of seconds. The application icon will increase somewhat, and wherever you move your finger, the application follows if you keep the finger down on the display screen. If you wish to move in one display of apps to some other display screen, simply move your finger to the edge of the iPad's screen and await the display to change.

- *Drop the application on another application icon*: You develop a folder by dragging an application onto another application you want in the same folder. Once you grab the app, you make a folder by dragging it together with another application you want in the same folder. When you hover together with the destination app, the application would blink once or twice and then broaden into a folder view. Drop the application within that new folder display screen to produce the folder.

- *Name the folder*: This is the third step that's not too necessary. The iPad gives the folder a default name like 'Video games,' 'Business' or 'Entertainment' when you create it, but if you would like a custom name for the folder, it is simple enough to edit. *First, you need to be in the folder view; you can leave a folder by clicking the Home button. On the home display, keep your finger on the folder until all the applications on display are jiggling. Next, lift your finger and then click the folder to increase it. The folder name near the top of the display screen can be edited by tapping into it.* After you have edited the name, click on the Home button to leave the 'edit' mode. You can add new applications to the folder using the very same method. Just grab the application and move it together with the folder. The folder would broaden just like it did when you initially created it, letting you drop the application anywhere inside the folder.

How to Remove an App From a Folder or Delete the Folder

You can remove an application from a folder by merely doing the reverse of what you did to generate the folder. You can also remove an application in one folder and drop it in another or even create a new folder from it.

Grab the app: You can grab and move applications around within a folder just as though the applications were on the home screen.

Drag the application from the folder: In folder view,

there's a curved box at the centre of the display that signifies the folder. If you pull the application icon out of the package, the folder will go away, and you'll be back again on the home display screen where you can drop the application icon anywhere you desire. This includes shedding it into another folder or hovering over another application to make a new folder.

The folder is deleted when the last application is deleted: So, if you would like to delete a folder, move every one of the apps from it and place them on the home display or in other folders.

Organize Your iPad Folder as You want

The best thing about folders is that, in lots of ways, they act exactly like app icons. This implies you can pull them in one screen to another or even move these to the dock. One cool way of arranging your iPad is to separate your applications into different categories, each using its folder, and you'll be able to move each one of these folders to your dock. This enables you to have indeed a single Home display screen that has usage of all your apps, or you can merely create one folder, name it 'Favorites' and then put your most used applications in it. After that, you can place this folder either on the original Home display or on your iPad's dock.

Chapter 9

iPad Exclusive Features

- *Benefit from Siri*

Siri isn't only for purchasing pizza or checking the elements; she is at her best when she's working as your assistant. Siri is quite with the capacity to maintain reminders, setting conference times, and scheduling occasions. She may also take a tone of voice dictation, and if you aren't useful with an on-screen keyboard but don't utilize it enough to buy a genuine keyboard, she'll do the massive raising for you. Siri could be the single most effective efficiency tool that is bundled with the iPad.

Siri works in mixture with the iPad's Calendar, Reminders, and other apps. These applications also sync through iCloud, and that means you can arrange a reminder on your iPad and also have it pop-up on your iPhone, and if multiple people use the same iCloud accounts, they'll all get access to those calendar occasions.

Here are some things Siri can do for you:

- "Remind me of the 9 AM Miller conference at 8:30 AM on Tuesday." This declaration will establish an 8:30 AM reminder in regards to a 9 AM meeting, which is convenient if you want to plan it.

- "Set up a meeting with Chris Miller tomorrow at 9 AM" which will stop off your calendar for 9 AM the very next day. The default event time is for just one hour; nevertheless, you can inform Siri how long it'll last.

- "Take a remember that the sizes of my table are 36

by 24." Don't want to bunch the Notes application and enter some quick information? Siri can do this too.

- <u>Download an Office Suite</u>

Among the little-known secrets about the iPad is, it possesses an office collection (apple's iWork), which includes Pages, Figures, and Keynote is free of charge download to whoever has bought an iPad or iPhone in the last couple of years. Thus, giving you the usage of an incredible selection of apps that will help with word control, spreadsheets, or presentations.

Do you like Microsoft Office? Additionally, it is designed for the iPad. Microsoft finally decided to stop banging their minds against the iPad teach and can get on the table instead. You can not only get Word, stand out, and PowerPoint, you can also download Perspective,

OneNote, Lync, and SharePoint Newsfeed. You can even download applications for Google Docs and Google Sheets that can make using Google's cloud-based tools easier.

- Integrate Cloud Storage

Talking about the cloud, Dropbox is one of the very most productive applications on the iPad. Not merely will it make burning your essential documents on the iPad simple, but additionally, it is excellent for focusing on both your iPad as well as your PC at precisely the same time. Dropbox can sync a document in seconds, which means you can go from going for a picture and making touch-ups on your iPad to performing a deeper coating of edits on your computer and then back again to your iPad in mere seconds. Dropbox isn't the only game around. There are a variety of excellent cloud storage space solutions for the iPad. And Apple has managed to get super easy to control cloud documents with the new Documents application and the drag-and-drop feature.

- Video Conferencing

It ought to be no real surprise that the iPad excels in marketing communications. You can also utilize it as a telephone, and between FaceTime and Skype, the iPad Pro 11vides quick access to video conferencing. But how about full-blown video conferences? Between Cisco WebEx Conferences and GoToMeeting, you will not have any moment collaborating, brainstorming, or just staying structured with a team of individuals.

- Scan Documents on Your iPad

The iPad's camera is entire with the capacity of performing as a scanning device, and because of lots of excellent apps, it is a breeze to have a picture of the record and also have that image clipped flawlessly such that it appears like it experienced a real scanning device. The very best part is most scanning device apps enable you to copy the record to cloud storage space, mark in the record, print it, and send it as a contact attachment.

Scanning device Pro is one of the best applications for scanning documents and utilizing; it could very well be more comfortable than making use of your camera. To scan a record, you tap the best orange "+" button, and the iPad's camera is triggered. All you have to do to check out the record is to align it within the camera's confines. Scanning device Pro will wait around until they have a decent shot and automatically snap the picture and crop it so that only the record shows up. Yes, it's that simple.

- <u>Buy an AirPrint Printer</u>

Let's remember printing; you can miss the gist that iPad

works with numerous different printers right from the package. AirPrint allows the iPad and printing device to communicate through an area Wi-Fi network, so there is no need for connecting the iPad to the computer printer. Buy a printing device that helps AirPrint, connect it to your Wi-Fi network, and the iPad will identify it.

You can print from within iPad applications by tapping the Share button, which appears like a box with an arrow appearing out of it. If the application works with printing, the "Printing" button can look in the next row of control keys in the Talk about the menu.

- Download the proper Apps

We've already protected most popular office suites for the iPad, and it might be impossible to list out all the great iPad applications that are of help in the workplace, but many can participate in almost any kind of work.

In case you need to take down notes, it goes beyond the actual built-in Notes application, and particularly if you need to talk about those records with other non-iOS devices, Evernote can be considered a real life-saver. Evernote is a multi-platform cloud-based version of Records.

Do you utilize a lot of PDF documents? GoodReader isn't just a terrific way to read them, but it will enable you to edit them. GoodReader connects to all or any of the ideal cloud storage space solutions, and that means you can plug it directly into your workflow.

Will you need to control jobs extend beyond the original iPad's reminders and calendar applications can offer? **Things** are one of the very best productivity applications on the iPad due to its superiority as an activity manager.

- Multitasking and Job Switching

After you have loaded your iPad up with great apps, you should navigate between those applications efficiently. Job Switching supplies the capability to quickly change between different applications seamlessly. You can activate Job Switching by double-clicking the home button to talk about the task display and tapping on the application you want to use. The iPad maintains the application in memory when it's in the backdrop such that it can be quickly packed when you activate it. You can even bring up the duty screen by putting four fingertips on the iPad's display screen and moving them toward the very best if you have multitasking gestures fired up in the iPad's configurations.

But the quickest way to change between tasks is to apply the iPad's dock. The brand-new dock gives you to place more icons onto it for fast access, but better still, it offers the last three applications you've opened up. These icons are on the much right part of the dock, plus they make it a breeze to switch in one app to another.

You can easily access the dock within any application by sliding your finger up from the bottom part of the display. Want to multitask? The dock can give you a hand there too. Rather than tapping the application icon to change to it, keep your finger down onto it. When you have an app open up and also you tap-and-hold an icon on the dock, you can pull it onto the medial side of the display screen. If both applications support multitasking, you will notice the full-screen application move to permit the new application to launch privately of the display. Once you've two applications up simultaneously, you may use the tiny divider between them to either allow them to each take up a fifty per cent of the display screen, one to operate on the medial side of the display or move the divider of the medial side of the display screen to close a multitasking app.

- <u>The 12.9-inch iPad Pro 11</u>

If you actually want to boost your efficiency, you should think about buying an iPad Pro 11. The difference between your iPad Pro 11 and the iPad Air (or "iPad") collection is vast. The iPad Pro 11 rivals most laptop computers in conditions of pure digesting power, it doubles the RAM within other iPads, and it gets the most advanced screen of any iPad, including support for wide-gamut colors.

But it's not only the speed that can make you more productive. The excess display space on the 12.9-inch model is ideal for multitasking. And if you execute a great deal of article marketing, the larger on-screen keyboard is approximately the same size as a regular keyboard. It even gets the row of quantity/symbol keys towards the top, conserving time from switching between different designs.

- <u>Learn How the professionals Navigate the iPad</u>

If you would like to become more productive on the iPad, you should become more efficient when using it. There are a variety of shortcuts in navigation that will help you get what your location is, faster. For instance, rather than trying to find an app, you can quickly release it by swiping down on the Home Screen to talk about Limelight Search and typing the application name into the search pub. You can even launch applications using Siri.

Also, utilize the task display screen. We've already discussed double-clicking the home button to talk about the task display. Even though you aren't switching backwards and forwards between apps, this is a superb way to start an app if you have used it lately.

- Add Websites to the Home Screen

If you frequently use specific websites for work, for example, a content management system (CMS), it can save you time with the addition of the web site to your iPad's Home Screen which allows the website to do something like any other app. And you will not believe how easy it is to save lots of the web site as an application icon. Demand web page, tap the Talk about button near the top of the display screen and choose "Increase Home Display" from the next row of options. The icon will become some other app, which means you can place it in a folder or even move it to the iPad's dock, which may give you fast access to it all the time.

- Dedicated Email Alongside Your Personal Computer

Sitting down in front of a desktop wouldn't make your iPad useless. The iPad can provide lots of great functions when you work; you can utilize it as an ardent email customer or instant message customer, or it can merely be utilized as fast access to the internet browser, which works better still if you have a dock for your iPad, rendering it almost like another monitor. And, yes, if you would like it to essentially act like yet another monitor, you can do so by installing an application like ***Duet Screen***.

- Buy a Keyboard

You have likely expected that one nearer to the very best of the list, but we recommend skipping the keyboard when buying an iPad. Many people are amazed at how quickly they can type using the on-screen keyboard, especially once they learn keyboard shortcuts like skipping the apostrophe and allowing AutoCorrect to place it. The iPad also helps you to dictate any moment the keyboard is on display by tapping the microphone button on a typical keyboard.

But if you will do a great deal of typing on the iPad, nothing at all beats a physical keyboard.

The iPad Pro 11 type of tablets supports Apple's Smart Keyboard, which might be the best overall keyboard for the iPad. One beautiful part about Apple keyboards is that Personal computer shortcuts like Command-C for duplicate will also focus on the iPad, helping you save from tapping on the display screen. And when utilized in mixture with the digital touchpad, it is nearly like utilizing a PC.

Don't possess an iPad Pro 11? You can even use Apple's Magic Keyboard with the iPad and get lots of the same features. The thing it will not do is charge through the iPad Pro 11's new connection.

CHAPTER 10

How to Secure iPad

On an iPad, you have a preference among a Custom Alphanumeric Code (that is a password with the use of letters and numbers), a Custom Numeric Code (figures only, however as many digits as you prefer!) or a 4-Digit Numeric Code (a fantastic old style pin!). You will need to decide which you need to use, so it is worth considering that earlier than you dive into the settings.

- Tap on the configuration icon, then scroll down and Tap on *Touch ID & Password*.

- In the **Touch ID** & Password menu, tap the blue hyperlink to turn Password ON.

- The default Security password placing is a Custom Alphanumeric Code - a complex password containing letters and digits. You could alternate this by tapping Password options.

- Tap your chosen password option to select it.

- Enter your **PASSWORD**. While you type in your secret four-digit, the display screen will increase automatically.

- Re-input your Security password to verify it. If the entered Passwords do not match, you might be returned to the first Security password access display to start over. If the Password that has been entered matches, then you will go back to the Security password menu.

- The final element to decide is how fast you want to enter your Password, which is often a balance between usability and safety. To change this setting, Tap **Require Password**.

- Pick your time out from the listing on screen by

tapping the interval you want to set. A tick will appear on that line, and when you're happy with the setting, tap Back at the very top left-hand nook.

You can allow access to certain functions of your iPad when the screen is locked. There are switches to enable the usage of *NOTIFICATIONS, SIRI*, and other components of the working gadget. Tap any of these to permit them (when **ON**, the switches can look green).

How to Set Up Touch ID to Unlock Your iPad

Now that you have set up a Password, you may want to enable **Touch ID**, which is fingerprint recognition to unlock your Devices (meaning you might not need to type in that password, even though you could if you want to!).

Follow the instructions below to achieve this effortlessly;

- To begin setting up **Touch ID**, you will want to be within the Settings **Menu.**

- In the predominant settings menu, select **Touch ID & Password.**

- Input your **Password** to access the settings.

- Tap **Add a Fingerprint**.

- To start including your fingerprint, place your finger or thumb onto the ***Home button***, however, do not press it. Lift and replace your finger as instructed on-screen, shifting it very slightly as you achieve this. When the center of your fingerprint has been scanned, you'll be requested to place your finger in unique positions on the home button to experiment the edges.

- While your fingerprint is fully scanned, you will

see the whole screen, displaying that your print has been captured and Touch ID is ready. Touch **Continue**.

- As you add fingerprints, they'll be numbered. You can change the names (so you recognize which print is which) or delete fingerprints from the phone by Tapping the name after which editing or deleting as required.

- When you've modified the name of fingerprint, Tap **Done** on the keyboard to keep the new name.

- **TOUCH ID** will be without delay activated for unlocking your iPad, and for **Apple Pay**. To enable iTunes and App Store Purchases to be authorized alongside with your fingerprint, Tap the switch to carefully turn it **ON,** then get into your Apple ID password.

You can upload as much as five Fingerprints, so putting

in place fingerprint access for your family members may be carried out too. A phrase of warning though; remember that in case you've introduced the capacity to use fingerprint scanning to authorize iTunes and App Store buys, anybody who's fingerprint is added can do this too!

CHAPTER 11

How to Activate used iPad

If you buy a used iPad, it is interesting. In the end, you come with an iPad and stretch your budget by acquiring a used one, especially for individuals who are not economically buoyant.

Some individuals encounter this issue along the way of activating their new device: The iPad will inquire further for somebody else's Apple ID and wouldn't typically work unless supplied.

This isn't a challenge that can't be fixed, so do not fret because you'll get it fixed following these steps.

- It is consequently an attribute of Apple's Find my iPad service known as activation lock.

- Activation Lock is a security measure that Apple raised to cope with the allergy of iPad thefts. In earlier years, if someone takes an iPad without blockage by lock feature, they could clean it, resell it, and breakout with the crime. Activation lock altered the situation.

- When the initial owner setup finds my iPad on the tool, the **Apple ID** used will be stored on Apple's activation servers together with almost every other information about the phone. The activation servers will most effectively unlock the phone again if that unique Apple ID can be used. If you no more have the Apple ID, you'll never be in a position to activate or use the tablet. This facilitates the security of your iPad because nobody would like to grab a tablet they can't use. On the other hand, it generally does not harm you if you recently procure the phone.

- Dealing with activation lock is annoying, but

additionally, it is smooth to solve. It's mainly possible, and the prior consumer just forgot to carefully turn off find my iPad or erase the tool correctly before offering it on the market (though it could also be a sign you've purchased a stolen device, so be cautious).

- You should contact the preceding owner of the telephone for him/her to consider the necessary steps.

How to Remove Activation Lock on iPad

- It is expedient that you should unlock or remove activation lock from the acquired iPad (used iPad) by inputting the prior owners' **Apple ID.** This technique can be initiated by getting in contact with the owner and detailing the scenario.

- If the owner lives near to you, I'll recommend that you hand over the phone back to him/her with the mission to insert the mandatory unlock code which is his/her Apple ID. When the seller gets the iPad at hand, he/she only will enter the necessary Apple ID on the activation lock display. Having done such, restart the telephone and then forge forward with the typical activation process.

Ways to Remove Activation Lock using iCloud

Sometimes, things can get a bit messy and complicated if the merchant/seller cannot physically access the tablet thanks to circumstances such as distance among other factors. This may also be resolved effortlessly as the owner may use iCloud to eliminate the activation lock from the phone through his accounts by following the steps below:

- Visit iCloud.com on any device, either mobile or laptop.

- Log-on with the Apple ID he/she used to activate the telephone.

- Click Find My iPad.

- Select All Devices.

- Go through the iPad you sold or want to market.

- **Select Remove from Accounts.**

Having achieved that, after that, you can PULL THE PLUG ON the iPad, and you switch it ON again. After that, you can proceed with the standard activation process.

How to Fix Locked Home-Screen or Security Password

If you activate your phone and find out either the iPad's home display screen or the security password lock display, therefore that the supplier/vendor didn't completely erase the smartphone before offering it for you. On this notice, you'll need the owner to wipe these devices to be able to do it with the activation process.

The next two procedures should be followed as you hand over the phone to the owner or seller to unlock the phone;

- If the tablet works on iOS 10 and later version, the owner has to log out of iCloud and subsequently erase these devices by heading *to Settings -> General -> reset -> Erase All Content* and *Settings.*

- If the tablet works on iOS 9, the seller/seller must go to *Settings -> General -> reset -> Erase All Content* and *Settings* and enter his/her Apple ID when prompted.

- When the erase process is completed, you're absolving to activate your phone with no further ado or hold off.

How to Wipe an iPad Using iCloud

Imagine if you can't gain access to the vendor/merchant due to some reasons, yet you will need your mobile phone to be wiped entirely for easy convenience, the seller may use iCloud to erase it. This is attained by ensuring the phone you want to get triggered linked to a WiFi network or mobile data network, and then inform the seller to follow along with the next steps:

- Visit http://iCloud.com/#find
- Sign in with the Apple id he/she applied to the phone that is with you or sold to you.
- Click *All Devices*.

- Choose the phone sold you or available to you.

- Select *Erase iPad.*

- When the phone is erased, click *Remove from Accounts.*

- Restart the phone, and you are all set.

How to Erase an iPad Using Find My iPad App

This process is very much indeed identical to the approach explained above using iCloud by just using the Find my iPad application installed on some other iPad device. If the owner prefers to get this done, connect the phone you're buying to Wi-Fi or mobile data, and then inform the owner to adhere to the steps below:

- Start the *find my iPad* app.

- Sign on with the Apple ID they applied to the phone sold

to you.

- Choose the phone.

- Tap *Actions*.

- Tap *Erase iPad*.

- Tap *Erase iPad* (It is the same button, however on a new display).

- Enter *Apple ID*.

- Tap *Erase*.

- Tap *Remove from Accounts*.

  - Restart the iPad and get started doing the setup process.

Chapter 12

8 Amazing iPad Shortcuts

- Put a supplementary application on the dock

The comfortable and straightforward shortcut isn't always decreasing, and that's true for the iPad. Do you realize you can press up to six applications on the dock at the bottom of the display? Which produces a great shortcut, letting you quickly release the app irrespective of where you are on your iPad. You can also put a folder on the dock, which really can become useful if you have many apps you utilize frequently.

- Using Spotlight Search to find apps

Speaking of starting apps, do you realize you can easily find an application without hunting through webpages and pages of the icon? The Limelight Search, which may be accessed by sliding your finger down while on the home screen, can help you find and start an app irrespective of where it is situated on your iPad. Enter the name, and then touch the app's icon when it seems in the results list.

- The Hidden Control Panel

Do you realize there's a hidden control panel with the usage of a few of the most typical settings? You can gain access to the control panel by swiping up from the bottom advantage of the iPad where in fact the screen matches the bevel. When you begin from this advantage and move your finger up, the control panel will reveal itself.

Typically, the most popular controls on this panel will be the music settings, which enable you to raise or lower the volume as well as skip songs; you can even use these settings to toggle Bluetooth on or off, change the iPad's Brightness or lock the rotation among other configurations.

- The Virtual Touchpad

One of the better additions to the iPad's operating-system within the last couple of years was the virtual touchpad. The iPad is just a little clumsy when working with the cursor, which is the positioning you are, in a stop of text; this is also true if you want to go completely left or right part of the display screen.

The virtual touchpad solves these problems by allowing the iPad's on-screen keyboard to do something as a touchpad when you have two fingers down onto it; this helps it be easy to go the cursor to a precise position in the written text or even to quickly spotlight a portion of text.

- Add Your Keyboard Shortcut

Sometimes, the auto-correct feature can obstruct you if you are typing on the iPad. But do you realize you can place it to do the job? In the iPad configurations under General and Keyboard is a button which allows you to include your shortcut. This feature enables you to enter a shortcut, such as your initials, and also have that shortcut replaced with a term, such as your name.

- Tremble to Undo

Talking about typing, do you realize there's a simple way to undo a grammatical error you've made? Exactly like PCs come with an edit-undo feature, the iPad also gives you to undo the last little bit of typing. Tremble your iPad, and it'll prompt you to verify if you want to undo the typing.

- Dividing the Keyboard into Two

If you're better typing with your thumbs than your fingertips, you will probably find the iPad's onscreen keyboard to be always a little too large. Luckily, there's a choice in the configurations to break up the iPad's keyboard in two, allowing easy access for your thumbs. Nevertheless, you won't need to hunt through your iPad configurations to find this specific feature. You can activate it by pinching out with your fingertips when you have the keyboard shown, which splits the keyboard into two halves on your display.

- Tap a Term to Get definition

Talking about reading articles on the net, do you realize you can easily research a word's description on your iPad? *Tap and hold before magnifying glass arises, and then lift your finger. A menu will pop-up asking if you would like to copy the written text to the clipboard or define the written text. Choosing define will provide you with a full description of the term. This feature also works in other applications like iBooks.*

- <u>Download Previously Purchased Apps</u>

Perhaps you have ever deleted an application and then decided you truly wanted it? Not merely will the iPad enable you to download previously purchased applications for free; however, the application store makes the procedure quite comfortable. Instead of searching for the common person application within the application store, you can pick the 'Purchased' tabs in the bottom of the application store to flip through all the apps you have purchased. There's a "Not on this iPad" tab near the top of the display screen that will thin it right down to applications you have erased.

Chapter 13

Fun Tricks You may not Know Your iPad can do

- <u>Create Your Movie Trailer or Edit Videos on your iPad</u>

When you get a new iPad (or iPhone), after a couple of years, you get access to the iWork and iLife collection of apps free of charge which consists of iMovie, which completely presents video editor that will help you to slice and splice video collectively from multiple videos, utilize features like sluggish movement and bring music into the video. Also, it has some really fun templates. When you release a fresh iMovie task, you receive the decision between developing a Movie, which enables you to work without a template, or a Trailer gives you fun options like a storybook, romance, etc.

- Watch TV on your iPad

There are a significant number of excellent applications for viewing movies on your iPad, but how about watching cable? There are many methods for you to get your preferred Television channels on your iPad, the best which include *Sling Television* and the *Sling Player*. Sling Television is an internet Television in the most literal sense, letting you stream stations to all of your devices. Sling Player is a little different. It works by intercepting your present wire broadcast and "slinging" it to your iPad. And they are just two of several ways to view Television on your iPad.

- Use Your iPad as another Monitor

This is an elegant trick; your iPad can be utilized as a digital monitor for your personal computer. Apps like

Duet Screen and ***Air Screen*** let you switch your tablet into a monitor. The capability to have two screens can do miracles for efficiency, and if you already own an iPad, there is no need to invest $200 or even more on another screen when cheaper alternatives can be found.

- Plug Your Acoustic guitar to the iPad

The *iRig and Gibson's GuitarConnect wire* are both great methods for getting installed, but once you have plugged your guitar into the iPad, you will want to take action with it. The iShredLive application works great alongside the GuitarConnect wire, and it even works together with Gibson's Stompbox, which enables you to control which results are active with a feet pedal. However, the Stompbox isn't quite as great as it appears, and another reliable way to get connected is through the *iRig, and IK Multimedia's AmpliTube,* and while you will not precisely be throwing out that Manager multi-effects bundle or junking all your feet pedals, the audio you escape these apps is in fact very good, if nearly stage-ready.

- Launch Apps Utilizing a Magical Incantation

So maybe the marvelous incantation sounds nearly the same as "Launch Email." It still seems as promised. **Siri** can be a potent tool that a lot of people avoid enough. Among the beneficial features is the capability to start apps. So, if you have ever hunted through display screen after display of application icons looking for Facebook, you could save lots of time by merely having Siri "release Facebook" for you.

You can even use Siri to try out music (a good playlist), dial a telephone number from your contacts or read your texts.

- Control Your Personal Computer Together with Your iPad

We've discussed making use of your iPad as another monitor, but how about controlling your computer with your iPad? Virtual Network Processing (VNC) is something which allows desktop posting and may be used to permit the iPad to regulate your personal computer's desktop. Two great applications that are appropriate for the VNC process are **Real VNC**, which enables you to have a test run free of charge, and **Parallels Access**, which makes Home windows on your iPad simpler to control via touch.

- Turn Siri Right into a Man or British

Does Siri's tone of voice grate on your nerves? You are not trapped with it. The British version of Siri includes both man and woman counterparts. Also, it has

American, Australian, and English accents.

You can transform the gender and accent by starting the Configurations app, choosing Siri from the left-side menu and tapping "Siri Tone of voice" towards underneath of the Siri options. And if you genuinely want some fun, you can transform Siri's vocabulary to start more options. The Language option is merely above Siri's tone of voice options.

- Suck Real Life Drawings into the iPad

The iPad's popularity has resulted in an excellent ecosystem of awesome accessories from an arcade cabinet that will turn your iPad into an old coin-operated game to real-world cars that are entirely managed by the iPad. *Osmo system* is among the coolest kid's accessories we have seen, which runs on the reflection and the iPad's camera to identify shapes and connect to real life in a distinctive way which enables your child to try out video games with the iPad without merely using the iPad display screen. Instead, they can attract front side of the iPad and also have their drawing connect to the objections on the screen, creating an entirely new way to try out and find out with the iPad.

How to Play the Guitar on iPad with iRig

iRig Features

- Gives you to plug your acoustic guitar into the iPad.

- Carries a pre-amp for improved tone.

- Free AmpliTube software includes amp simulation and with two results: Noise Filtration system and Delay.

- Distortion impact is free with registration.

- Additional effects range between $2.99 to $4.99

- The iRig and AmpliTube Combine to produce a Great Results Processor

The iRig enables you to plug your guitar into the iPad and utilize it as an amp simulator. You can also output the audio to your headphones, exterior loudspeakers, a PA system, or even your electric guitar amplifier; and going hand-in-hand with *iRig* is AmpliTube, an application from *IK Multimedia* that may be downloaded from the application store. AmpliTube provides different results like delay, sound decrease, and distortion, and you may purchase more results within the app, including chorus, wah, and phaser. These results range in cost from $2.99 to $4.99, which is a significant saving in comparison to purchasing the actual pedals, and the outcome turns your iPad into a virtual results pedalboard. But there is undoubtedly more to Amplitube than only an effects bundle. It offers an acoustic guitar tuner, a metronome, and a recorder, with a choice for buying an 8-monitor recorder. As well as perhaps the best feature is the capability to import tunes from your iTunes library, play along with them, and even duplicate these to a monitor on the 8-monitor. Having trouble learning a specific riff? You can also slow the song down and invest some time on it.

There's a lot to like about the **iRig**, and you start with the sound. The adapter includes a preamp, which gives an immaculate sound of good quality to AmpliTube. Even though you will not mistake the distortion pedal within the app with a good pedal, it'll contend with most multi-effects deals. For the purchase price, the iRig is challenging to defeat, and for individuals who want to bring their results and amp along with them without lugging a great deal of gear almost everywhere, it's a good deal.

- AmpliTube's Small Annoyances Won't Slow You Down

The thing we'd change about the iRig itself is the cord; measuring only six inches, it's way too short. We'd much favor the option to have the iPad through to a desk and the adapter on the floor.

AmpliTube is a different tale; the sound it produces is fantastic considering you are paying several dollars for a results pedal that may set you back $100 at the music store. However, the user interface lacks the same elegance. The many knobs you'll encounter on your simulated amp, and results packages won't enable you to properly twist them, even though you can add an impact to a slot machine, you can't pull an effect in one slot to another. So, if you would like to add sound reduction to the very best of the order, you need to set up everything again.

Chapter 14

iPad Tips and Keyboard Shortcuts

- <u>iPad On-Screen Keyboard Shortcuts</u>

Perhaps the easiest way to increase typing on the on-screen keyboard is to learn most of the various little tricks and shortcuts that can make the whole process considerably faster.

- At the end of a sentence, you can tap the area bar twice in a row, and the iPad would output an interval, an area, and turn the caps key ON, so you are prepared for another sentence.

- There's no dependence on an apostrophe in your contractions when you have an automated spelling corrector. You can type "Im" for "I'm" and "cant" for "can't" and allow iPad to do the excess job.

- With an iPad Pro 11, you can type those unique icons above the figures by swiping down on the principal element or holding your finger down on the main element to make a pop-up window with the particular sign.

- Here's an excellent keyboard technique for placing something in quotation marks: tap and hold the question tag/period key on the standard layout for twice quotes, or if you would like single quotes, touch and hold the exclamation/comma key.

- Need special accents? You may get at distinctive highlight marks for specific vocabulary support by tapping and keeping the corresponding notice key.

- Do you realize you can place begin estimates and end quotations? On the amounts layout, just tap and hold the quotation key for starting and ending rates. Tap and hold the solitary estimate key for the same options for one quote. You can even reach a highlight using this system on the lone quotation key.

- On the quantities design, you can tap and contain the exclamation tag for an ugly exclamation tag and the question tag for an ugly question tag. But for individuals who love their pauses, the decision trick is keeping down the time key on the layout of the figure to access an ellipsis.

- Sick and tired of flipping backwards and forwards from characters to numbers? Rather than tapping the "123" key to access the numbers, keep your finger down onto it and then slip your finger to the main element you will need. When you release your finger, the iPad will produce your personality and automatically turn back to the initial keyboard layout.

- You can even do the tap and hold technique on the shift key to quickly get a capital letter.

- Create Your Keyboard Shortcut! You don't need to rely just on these pointers. Apple helps it be easy that you should create your shortcuts on the iPad's keyboard.

- <u>Remember the Shortcut Control Keys Together with The Keyboard</u>

If you look above the very best line of words, you will notice some shortcut keys. Around the remaining part, two arrows curve into fifty percent circles. The arrow that curves left can be an undo key, that may undo the last change you made to a record. The arrow that curves to the right is a redo key that will 'undo' a redo action. Towards the right of these two control keys is a button that appears like a bit of paper before a clipboard, which is the paste button. You can utilize it to paste whatever is on the digital clipboard into the document.

On the far side of the keyboard are additional control keys. The "BIU" button enables you to *bold, italicize, and underline* text messages. The camera button enables you to gain access to your camera move to paste an image, and the paper clip provides up iCloud Drive, letting you attach a document to the record. You may even have a squiggly collection that is utilized for creating an instant drawing.

These shortcut control keys will not continually be present. For instance, if the application you have open up doesn't support accessories, the paper clip button won't appear.

- Don't Type: Dictate!

Do you realize the iPad helps voice dictation? It could be easily the best keyboard alternative feature on the iPad. The tone of voice dictation is one of the numerous tricks **Siri** is capable of doing, and you may be amazed at how accurate it is, not forgetting how considerably faster it could be in comparison to typing.

You can begin dictating by tapping the microphone button next to the area bar on the on-screen keyboard. You can even use voice instructions like "new paragraph" and dictate unique icons like "quotation tag" or "exclamation tag." Once you get accustomed to it, the tone of voice dictation can be considered a significant time-saver.

- Use Predictive Typing to Increase Content Input

Predictive typing is one of the coolest & most easily overlooked features put into the on-screen keyboard lately. Among the shortcut control keys together with the keyboard are areas for three different predictions. As you type, the iPad will attempt to guess the term.

It's an excellent habit to understand these predictions, particularly when tapping in longer words. An instant tap of the prediction button can save a great deal of hunting and pecking. Also, you ought to know of the prediction with quotes around it. This enables you to skip any attempt to auto-correct your text message and can keep it similar as you've typed it.

You can even turn Auto-Correct off, which is often a lifesaver if you enter a great deal of jargon the iPad doesn't identify. When Auto-Correct is switched off, you have control over the corrections. Misspelled words remain highlighted, and if you touch them, you are offered options to improve the word.

- <u>Use a Custom Keyboard Like Swype or SwiftKey</u>

Swype and *SwiftKey* are third-party keyboards that enable you to 'type' words without lifting your finger. Instead, you glide from notice to notice. It sounds uncomfortable; nevertheless, you would be astonished at how quickly you feel familiar with it. The much longer you utilize these keyboards, the quicker your hands memorize the gestures for simple words, accelerating your content access even further.

Not everyone prefers these gliding keyboards, but many people swear by them. To be able to install one of the keyboards, you must first download the application from the App Store and then allow the keyboard in the Keyboard configurations under "General" configurations in the iPad's configurations Settings. If it noises just a little complicated, it is. Nonetheless, it is simple enough to do if you follow our instructions for setting up a third-party keyboard.

Most third-party keyboard applications also offer you instructions about how to set up them if you release the keyboard application directly.

- Shortcuts on the Smart Keyboard and Bluetooth Keyboard

The Smart Keyboard designed for the iPad Pro 11 adds a command key and a choice key, much like keyboards created for the Mac pc. (Home windows users can think of them as like the control and alt secrets). By iOS 9, the iPad works with keyboard shortcuts using certain key combinations. These shortcuts will continue to work using the Smart Keyboard, Apple's Cellular Keyboard & most Bluetooth keyboards which have the control and option tips.

Here are some useful shortcut combinations:

- Command-B, Command-I, and Command-U for daring, italics, and underline.

- Command-N for new documents: a fresh note in Records, a new message in Email, etc.

- Command-F for finding text message within the document

- Command-R to reply to an email

- Command-T to open up a new tab in Safari

- Command-W to close a tab in Safari

- Command-Tab showing the next tabs in Safari.

How to Force-Quit or Close an iPad App

- *How exactly to Force-Quit an App?*

Open up the multitasking and control display by double-clicking the home button at the bottom of your iPad. The home button is the physical button just underneath the iPad's screen that you utilize for Touch ID. You can even use Multitasking gestures by pinching along with 4 or 5 fingertips anywhere on the display screen.

The App Switcher can look with recently opened iPad applications displayed as windows over the screen. Each window features an icon above it combined with the name. You can even slip your finger from left to right and scroll through new apps, so if the application involved isn't your lately used, you can still reach it.

Keep your finger on the application window you want to close and then glide your finger to the very best of the display without ever raising your finger from the iPad's screen. This gesture would turn off the app. Think about it as "flicking" the windowpane from the iPad.

- <u>Imagine if Closing the App Doesn't Resolve the Problem?</u>

The next phase, after force-quitting an application, is rebooting the iPad. When you click on the rest/wake button near the top of these devices, the iPad will go to rest. To restart the iPad, hold the rest/wake button down for mere several seconds until you start to see the instructions to "slip to power down" the iPad. Follow these instructions and wait around before the iPad's display will go dark before clicking the rest/wake button to power it ON again.

If you're having trouble with a particular application and rebooting doesn't solve it, you should attempt deleting the application and then download it again from the App Store. You will not have to cover the application to reinstall it. However, you will eventually lose whatever you have saved in the application unless the application will save it to the cloud-such as Evernote saving your records to the Evernote servers.

- Do I have to Always Force-Quit Apps?

The iOS environment knows if you are using an application or require it to work in the background. When you change, iOS tells the application it has a couple of seconds to summarize what it's doing. Similarly, the application can continue what it's focusing on before it will go inactive, and iOS will give those applications the digesting power they want.

Apps like Apple Music can play music even though they're inactive. They'll keep doing this if you don't force-quit or go back to them and stop the playback. For all the apps, when you change to some other app, iOS suspends the main one you were utilizing, and it halts getting resources like the processor chip, screen, loudspeaker, etc.

You certainly do not need to force-quit applications unless the application misbehaves.

CHAPTER 15

How to Extend iPad's Battery Life

With every iPad release, one continuous point remains. The iPad is now faster, and the images get better every year. Nevertheless, the device works with the first 10 hours of battery life. However, also for those individuals that use their iPad 24hrs each day, it's still easy for it to perform. Moreover, there is nothing worse than looking to stream video from Netflix and then have that low battery message pop-up and interrupt your show.

Thankfully, there are a few tips you could utilize to keep iPad battery life and hold that from happening as often.

Concealed secrets that will change you into an iPad expert:

Right here's how you can get the best of your iPad's battery life span:

- **Adjust the brightness:** The iPad comes with an automatic-brightness feature which facilitates the iPad predicated on the light quality within the area, but this program isn't always enough. Modifying the overall lighting could be the first solitary thing you can do to help ease out a little more from your battery consumption. You can transform the light by starting the iPad's configurations, choosing screen & view from the left-side menu and moving the brightness slider. The goal is to get it to a stage where it's nevertheless comfortable enough to learn, however nearly as shiny as the default establishing.

- **Switch off Bluetooth:** Most of us haven't any Bluetooth devices linked to the iPad, so all the Bluetooth carrier does for all of us is waste charge of the iPad's battery life. When you have no Bluetooth devices connected, ensure Bluetooth is switched off. A brief way to turn the transfer for Bluetooth off is to open up the iPad manager - panel by swiping up from the backside of the screen.

- **Switch off Location services:** At precisely the same time as even the Wi-Fi version of the iPad will do a fantastic job of identifying its location, most people do not use the location service on our iPad as much as we utilize them on our iPad. Turning OFF GPS is a concise and clean manner to save lots of a little battery even while not quitting any feature. Also, remember if you need to use GPS, you may switch it **ON**. You can switch off location services in the iPad's configurations below privacy.

- **Turn off notification:** While notification is an excellent feature, it can drain a small amount of battery life because the tool assessments to check on if it needs to force a notification to the screen. If you want to do the most to optimize your battery life, you can turn drive notification off completely. You could likewise turn it off for specific apps, reducing all of the push notifications you obtain. You may switch off notification in configurations.

- **Fetch email less regularly:** With default configurations, the iPad will check out brand spanking new email each quarter-hour. Pushing this back to a half-hour or one hour can help your battery last much longer. Move to configurations, choose the email settings and select the "fetch new data" choice. This will enable you to set how often your iPad fetches email. There could even be a choice only to have check email manually.

- **Switch off 4G:** More often than not, we use the iPad at home, this means the use from it via our mobile data connection on. We utilize it at home exclusively. If you regularly end up low on battery, a good suggestion is to turn off your 4G data connection. This may protect it from draining any power when you are not using it.

- **Turn off background application refresh:** Background app refresh keeps your apps up to date by relaxing them even while the iPad is idle or as long as you're on various other apps. This may drain a little extra battery strength. Get into configurations, choose General configurations and scroll down till you find "background app refresh." You can choose to turn off the service or certainly flip off specific apps you don't want to run in the background.

- **Discover apps consuming your battery:** Do you realize you could test thoroughly your iPad's battery usage? That is a fantastic manner to find what applications you're using the most and which apps can be consuming more than their expected percentage of your battery. You could test utilization within the iPad's configurations by choosing battery from the left-hand side menu.

- **Match iPad improvements:** It's continuously important to keep iOS updated to the latest from

Apple. Not merely would this help optimize the battery life of the iPad, it also ensures you're getting the latest security fix and patching any bugs that have popped up, which allows the iPad run efficiently.

- **Reduce Animation:** That is a technique to save a little of battery life and make the iPad show up a bit more reactive. The iPad's user interface consists of a few animations like glass windows zooming in and zooming out, and the parallax influence on icons, which makes them seem to hover over the backdrop picture. You can turn off those user interface effect by heading to **Settings**, Tapping **General Settings**, Tap **Display,** and getting to reduce animation to get it turned **Off**.

- **Buy a Smart Case:** The smart case can save battery life by placing the iPad into **Sleep mode** when you close the flap. It might not look like a great deal of conservation, however in case you aren't with the habit of striking the rest/wake button each time you have completed using the iPad; it could help offer you a supplementary five, ten or even quarter-hour extension of battery strength by the end of the day.

CHAPTER 16

How to Fix iPad that won't Charge

If you're having troubles charging your iPad when it's linked to your personal computer, you are in good company. While your iPad or iPod device might not have a difficulty charging when connected to the USB slot on your pc, the iPad requires substantially higher power. This means that some USB slots, especially the ones on old computer systems, genuinely don't have the feature to get the duty performed.

How to know if your iPad is charging

If the device has enough power to charge the iPad, a lightning bolt can be shown within the center of the battery meter at the very top right-hand corner of the iPad.

If it generally does not have enough capacity to charge the iPad, you might start to see the phrases "not charging" next to the battery meter.

Usually, the iPad can be charged using the computer if you positioned it in active mode. However, if the computer is set into sleep mode, the iPad will not charge.

The smooth and straightforward answer is to plug the iPad into a power outlet by using the adapter that is included with the iPad. That's also the quickest way to charge the iPad. Even personal computers that could effectively charge the iPad may not place out almost as much current as a standard charger. Some power strips additionally have USB ports to charge USB devices, which may be an incredible manner to charge the iPad.

Trouble charging the iPad when Connected to Power Outlet

First, be sure the iPad does not have a software problem by rebooting it. To achieve that, press down the sleep button on the top right-hand corner of the iPad. After some mere seconds, a crimson button can appear instructing you to slip it to the power of these devices.

Allow it shut down completely, and then click the power button down to power ON. You might start to see the apple brand logo appear at the center of the screen even while it boots up.

If the iPad still doesn't charge using the electrical outlet, you may have to check your cable or the adapter. You could discover if you have trouble with the cable by linking the iPad to your laptop with the cable.

If you start to see the lightning bolt on battery meter or

"not charging" next to the battery meter, you know the wire is working. If this is the case, absolutely buy a new adapter.

If the computer will not respond when you plug in the iPad, it is then not recognizing the iPad connected, meaning the issue is possibly with the cable.

In rare circumstances, while changing the adapter and the cable will not do just fine, you might have a hardware issue with the iPad. If so, you'll need to contact Apple for support. (If you live near an Apple Store, try getting in touch with the customer support. Apple Store staff can be quite accommodating.)

CHAPTER 17

How to Watch TV for Free on iPad

Among the exquisite issues about the iPad is for you to use the Tablet for viewing TV. There are a few appropriate alternatives that support you to view Television on your iPad, and that means you don't have to miss your preferred show or any big game.

Many of these devices functions by intercepting its transmission out of your wire package and then broadcasting it through your wi-fi network, that enables you to access your shows from any place in the home even though on the run via your iPad's data connection.

However, one thrilling option converts the iPad into a lightweight TV, and if you do not want to invest the money on expensive add-ons or accessories, sometimes an application is all you have to.

TiVo Stream

If you're not thinking about cutting the cable, TiVo could be the best answer for pressing your television sign to your iPad. Sadly, it might be the most luxurious, at least beforehand charges. You'll either want to include a TiVo stream device on your existing TiVo set up, or you will require the TiVo Roamio Plus, which include both TiVo Roamio for essential TiVo supplier and the TiVo motion for loading throughout the internet.

However, while getting set up on TiVo is more expensive, you might forestall renting an HD Dvd movie recorder from your wire issuer, which may be helping you save money.

The huge bonus to TiVo stream is the ability to watch recorded shows in addition to concert events. The flow fundamentally turns your iPad into a TiVo player, which means you get access to the whole great deal documented on your TiVo's DVR.

@TV Plus

Belkin is the newest manufacturer to leap into the market place, and their @TV is priced among the volcano glide and the Slingbox Slingplayer. It offers all precisely the same primary functions of both products, which include the ability to pause and record live TV.

One feature oddly lacking from @TV can be an HDMI connection. @TV best uses an element or amalgamated cables instead of the better acceptable HDMI.

Cable Television / Network Apps

A chance to starting up hardware on your entertainment device or plugging an antenna into the iPad is downloading applications from your Wire Company or primary networks.

Many major companies like COX TV, Time Warner Cable, and DirectTV offer applications for the iPad, and that means you can watch TV, even though not all support the full total range of TV provided through your subscription rather than all provision ability to stream over 3G/4G/5G.

You could additionally access top-class articles via apps, with a few restrictions based on your issuer. HBO, Cinemax, Showtime and Starz all have applications that utilize a few providers.

Beyond reputable applications from your wire issuer or top quality channels, there are a few remarkable applications for streaming films and TV. The two most popular choices are **Netflix**, which gives an excellent selection of movies and Television for a comparatively low subscription charge, and **Hulu Plus**, which doesn't have precisely the same movie series but offers a few Television shows still within the present-day season.

Crackle is likewise an excellent choice for loading movies and will not require any membership charges.

Slingbox Slingplayer

No more to be confused with Sling TV, Slingbox's Slingplayer works via intercepting the TV signal away off your wire box and "slinging" it across your home network. The Slingplayer software transforms one's body into a good deal that enables you to stream it to your iPad across both Wi-Fi as well as your iPad's 3G/4G/5G data connection. Using the Slingplayer app, you can listen to other stations watching any television screen that you can view at home. You can also gain access to your DVR watching recorded shows.

Beyond being truly a very significant way to view remotely, Slingplayer is also an incredible solution for people who want usage of the television in virtually any room inside without connecting wire or springing for two televisions. One drawback would be that the iPad application should be bought individually and provides an incredible chunk onto the charge of these devices.

Sling TV

The war to cut the cord has been waging for a couple of years now, but when sling TV surfaced, the tide officially started to be towards the cable companies. Sling TV is not a tool that throws your current day cable indicators to your Television or an antenna that accumulates channels for your iPad. It's an online cable company, due to this, they do precisely the same simple process that your wire organization will, without strolling wire to your dwelling.

Instead, you stream your channels throughout the internet. Sling provides you with the usage of popular stations like ESPN, AMC, TNT, TBS as well as others. You can additionally sign up to HBO, Epix, and further channel packages.

The very best part is that sling TV needs to forget about hardware to work. The terrible part is that it will not broadcast local stations.

Chapter 18

Advance iPad Tips

The iPad is an excellent tablet, yet most users have no idea about all the useful tips and shortcuts that makes life more facile with it. New iOS improvements are continuously adding cool new features, and that means you can be left outdated unless you know everything your iPad could probably do for you. We'll help you learn some of these critical features here.

- <u>Find applications quickly</u>

How will you find a specific application you installed on your iPad when you have lots of apps? Don't spend your time flipping through the displays; instead, use the iPad's Limelight search, which may be accessed by swiping down on the screen. Once you get accustomed to searching the iPad, you will not know how you'd be patience to do it some other way; you can even use this solution to search through your contact or even your email.

- Miss/skip the apostrophe when typing

The iPad's autocorrect will often get on your nerves, but at other times it really can be excellent. If you type a great deal, you'll without a doubt need to use the apostrophe regularly, mainly when you are typing in a contraction like "can't" or "won't"; do you realize you can miss the apostrophe? *The best iPad typing suggestion is using the autocorrect to improve "can not" to "can't" and "will not" to "won't."*

- Quick onscreen music controls

The iPad has buttons privately for changing the volume, but think about skipping a song? You don't have to release the music application to miss a track. The iPad's control panel enables you to do things such as adjusting the lighting of the display screen, turn off/on the Bluetooth, and even reach the timer. *Slip your finger up from the bottom part of the display. You can pause, play, or forward or backwards.*

- Connect your iPad to your HDTV

You aren't limited by the iPad's screen if you are watching a movie or playing a casino game. You can even connect the iPad to an HDTV. The simplest way is through Apple Television, which facilitates Air-Play and enables you to wirelessly cast your iPad's display screen to your Television. But even though you have no desire for Apple TV, you can purchase an adapter to plug your iPad into the TV. *The very best solution is Apple's Digital AV Adapter; nevertheless, you can also get composite or component cables.*

- Divide the safari browser in two

You may need a newer/latest iPad to utilize this tip. The iPad Air 2, iPad Mini 4, and iPad Pro 11 or more modern tablets can start using a break-up view feature with the Safari internet browser. This splits the web browser into two home windows hand and hand, that allows you to see two websites at the same time. As the iPad requires a little elbow room because of this one, you must be keeping the iPad in scenery mode.

To enter break up view in the Safari internet browser, tap and contain the Webpages button: the button in the upper-right part of the Safari display that appears like a square within another square. When you click this button, you will notice all your open webpages, but when you possess your finger down onto it, a menu shows up that gives you the decision of opening divide view (if your iPad facilitates it), opening a new tab, or shutting all your Safari tabs.

If you are in a break-up view, this menu appears at the bottom of the screen. *To summarize divided view, do a similar thing: keep down the Web pages button to get the choice to combine all tabs.*

- Use a custom keyboard

Instead of skipping the apostrophe when typing, another option is installing a brand-new screen keyboard on your iPad; given that widgets are backed, you can use a custom keyboard. These keyboards come with many different advantages, like the capability to attract words by maintaining your finger pressed against the screen while moving from notice to letter, a method that sounds unusual but actually will save lots of time. You can use a third-party keyboard by downloading one from the App Store and turning it on in the iPad's keyboard configurations.

- <u>Add applications to the home screen bottom level tray</u>

The iPad includes four applications underneath the tray of the home screen, but do you realize you can include up to six applications to it? You can also take away the ones that are there by default and add your own.

Touch and hold an application icon until all the applications start shaking; this enables you to go through applications around by dragging them with your finger. To get an application into the bottom level tray, pull it down and drop it on the holder. You will see the other applications move to make room for this, and that tells you it is alright to drop it.

Pro Suggestion: You can drop entire folders into the bottom level tray too. If you have a couple of video games, you always want fast access, to simply put all of them in a folder and then drop the folder in this tray.

- Organize your applications with folders

While using Limelight to find apps is fantastic, typing within an app name every time you want to gain access to it might not be for you. Folders enable you to reach apps with a few taps or swipes; you should use folders to easily organize your iPad and individual apps into customized categories. The iPad will generate a default folder name that is usually a pretty good explanation of the applications it includes; nevertheless, you can rename the category to whatever you want.

To make a folder, *hold your finger down on an app's icon until all the apps start to tremble. Next, move the app together with another app, and the iPad will generate a folder made up of the apps.* To include more applications to the folder, pull them over, and drop them on the recently created folder.

As stated earlier, you can move folders to underneath tray; you should use this to make a menu-system of types containing your preferred applications by dragging multiple folders to the holder. You can also arrange your iPad so that the majority of your applications are stored in folders lined over the bottom level tray as well as your most-used applications are on the first web page of the home screen.

- The iPad's virtual Touchpad can make you forget your mouse

Do you realize there is a virtual touchpad included in your iPad? This touchpad might not be as effective as genuine, but it's close. You can use it any moment the on-screen keyboard shows up. Keep two fingertips down on the keyboard and move them around the screen; you will notice a triggered. As you move your fingertips around the display screen, the cursor will move with them. If you click and keep an item before moving your fingertips, you can also select text message this way, and you don't have to tap your fingertips on the real keyboard because of this to work. You can touch two fingertips anywhere on the display to activate the touchpad.

- Reboot the iPad

Do you realize you can solve many issues with the iPad by merely rebooting it? *Is your iPad operation slow? Reboot it. Will an application quit each time you start it? Reboot it.*

Unfortunately, you can confuse placing the iPad into

suspend mode with a hard reboot. To necessarily give your iPad a brand-new start, you can reboot it by pursuing these quick steps:

1. *Press down the Rest/Wake button at the same time as pressing the home button*: maintain these for a couple of seconds. The iPad will go empty as it shuts down.

2. *Press down the Rest/Wake button again as it starts booting up*: When you start to see the Apple logo design show up, you can release the Rest/Wake button. The iPad's home display screen can look momentarily.

- <u>Save battery life by turning down display brightness</u>

An instant way to save your iPad's electric battery is to lessen the display screen brightness. You can do this by locating the iPad's configurations and choosing Screen & Brightness from the left-side menu. (When you have a mature iPad, the choice may be called Brightness & Wallpaper.) You can move the slider to change the Brightness. Adjust the slider to improve the light of the display, the dimmer the screen; the less battery it uses.

- Disable in-app purchases

A very important factor every parent ought to know how to do is "switching off in-app buys on the iPad." Usually, that seemingly free game may finish up, costing a massive amount of money; after your seven-year-old purchases, a couple of in-game costs might increase to $4.99 a touch. It's pretty easy to prevent this; first, you will need to *allow parental settings by locating your iPad's configurations and choosing General from the left-side menu. On this display, find Limitations. In the*

Limitations/Restriction menu, you will have to enable limitations, that may ask you for a four-digit passcode.

Once you've enabled these parental handles, it is only a matter of scrolling listed below until you start to see the option for In-App Buys. When you glide this to the Off position, most applications won't even show the display screen for purchasing items, and the ones that do will be avoided from going right through with any transactions.

- Control your personal computer from your iPad

Want to consider things a step further? It is possible to control your personal computer from your iPad. This works on both Windows-based PCs and Macs. *You need to install software on your computer as well as an application on your iPad, but it is simple to manage it.* There are a bunch of excellent free software option you can get online, although if you intend on utilizing it extensively, you might like to go with paid tools.

CHAPTER 19

How to Fix a Slow iPad Tablet

Is your iPad working slowly? Might it get bogged down after a couple of hours? At the same time as this is extra, not uncommon with old iPads that don't have the control power of the new iPad Air and iPad Pro 11 Tablets, even the latest iPad can impede. A couple of multiple reasons just why an iPad could also begin operating slow, such as an application having troubles or a sluggish web connection. Thankfully, that is generally easy to revive.

- **First: stop all of your new apps**

One common reason behind an iPad to start chugging is a problem with the application itself instead of the iPad. If you enjoy a form that is working slower than usual, it could sound reasonable to go through the home button to close the application and re-launch it. However, pressing the home button wouldn't normally close out the app. It suspends the app, which mostly keeps it freezing in the backdground.

Some applications even continue steadily to run in the backdrop mode. Those are usually applications that stream music like Pandora, Spotify, or the melody app that is included with the iPad.

If the hassle is specifically with an individual app, we'll need to stop from it using the duty display. This may correctly close the application down and purge it from memory space, permitting you to release a 'fresh' version from it. Please discover that you might lose unsaved functions by exiting the app. If it's currently working on an objective, it could be better to make the application finishes the duty before proceeding.

Within the job screen, it is an excellent concept to have a

summary of any applications that are taking part in music. It's not likely they may be causing a headache, or even if the application is loading the track from the web, it will not expend enough of your bandwidth to rely upon. However, last from the app won't hurt, and maybe sure the application isn't impacting something.

To shut the program, you will need to constitute a summary of all apps that will be operating in the background.

- **Double-click the home button in the bottom of your iPad**.

When you press it two times in quick succession, your most up to date applications are shown as cascading home windows across the screen. You might navigate via this screen by swiping from left-to-right or right-to-left. The windows can have a related application icon above it.

***To close an app:

- Keep the finger down at the home display window.

- Without lifting your finger from the screen, swipe in the direction of the very best of the screen.

***This gesture resembles "*flicking*" the application from the iPad. Remember: you Tap the application windowpane, not the application icon.

Reboot the iPad

Closing the applications may not continuously do just fine. Within this example, rebooting the iPad is the product quality recourse. This will flush from memory and offer your iPad a fresh start.

NB: many humans believe the iPad forces down as the rest/wake button on the top right-hand corner of the iPad is pressed down or as the flap of their smart cover or bright case is closed, but this places the iPad in droop/suspend setting.

To reboot the iPad:

- Keep down the rest/wake button until instructions appear; letting you know to glide a button to power from the iPad.

- When you slip the button, the tablet will turn off, and the iPad's screen should go dark.

Wait around several seconds and then start the iPad up pressing down the rest/wake button once again. You'll first start to see the Apple brand logo design on the screen as well as your iPad need. Your iPad must run extra fast but, if it begins bogging down, retain in mind the apps that are running at that time. Once in a while, a single application can purpose the iPad to execute poorly.

Is your iPad still walking slower than you want?

Check your wireless connection

It could not be your iPad that is working sluggishly. It could be your mobile network.

You can attempt the internet speed of your Wi-Fi network by using an application like *Ookla's Speedtest*. This application will send information to a remote server and then dispatches records back to the iPad, looking into each send and download rates of speed.

The usual Wi-Fi network in the U.S. Gets around 12 megabits-per-second (Mbps), though it is unusual to see rates of speed of 25+ Mbps. You possibly might not see plenty of the slowdown using your connection until it receives around 6 Mbps or significantly less. It is across the amount of bandwidth it requires to stream films and video.

If you're experiencing a headache with your Wi-Fi

connection, try moving nearer to your router. If the pace increases, you might look at improving your Wi-Fi range. That's common in more prominent structures, but even a little home could have troubles.

Ensure you're updated to the latest version of iOS

iOS is the operating device working on the iPad. At precisely the same time as the best revise sometimes will positively sluggish the iPad down a little, it's always a great idea to perform the latest operating-system on device. Not handiest will this make sure that you have the most up to date efficiency tweaks, it additionally warranties you have present fixes for just about any protection problems.

Setup an ad-blocker

If you're mainly seeing a decline when surfing the

internet in the safari internet browser, however, your web velocity is not sluggish, with the ability to be more an indicator of which webpages you're surfing than the iPad itself.

The more significant advertisements with a web page, the much longer it does take to load. Moreover, if some of those advertisements stall out, you might be left anticipating the web page to pop-up.

One fashion to this is to set up an advertisement blocker. Those widgets beautify the safari web browser by using disallowing advertisements to weight on the internet website. They make each for more straightforward reading and faster launching. Sites such as this one generate income from adverts, which means this is a balance you have to fight.

Flip off background app refresh

Background app refresh let applications to refresh their content even when you are not utilizing them. In this manner, Facebook might Tap base and retrieve articles in your post wall, or an information app may also fetch the newest articles.

However, this runs on your processing rate and your web connection, so that it can make the iPad to perform just a little slower. This usually isn't the theory cause, but if you frequently find the iPad working slow (and if the electric battery drains quickly), you must flip off background app refresh.

Showing off background application refresh:

- Head to your iPad's configurations.

- Choose **General** from the left-hand navigation menu.

- Tap the background application refresh.

- Tap the on/off slider near the top of the screen.

If you are nevertheless experiencing progressive speeds, there is certainly yet another factor you can do.

Clear STORAGE SPACE

If you're operating desperately low on space for storage, clearing up a little more room for the iPad can on occasion, improve efficiency. This will be achieved by deleting applications that you haven't used for quite a long time, particularly video games you don't play anymore.

It's clean to see which applications are employing the most space on your iPad:

1. Head to **Settings.**

2. Select **General** from the left-hand navigation

menu.

3.   Tap **storage space & iCloud usage**.

4.   Tap **Manage Storage Space** (under the very best storage program). This may demonstrate which apps are using up the utmost storage.

You can additionally increase safari when you delete your cookies and internet background, although this might purpose you to log back to any websites that have saved your login records.

CHAPTER 20

How to Fix iPad Pro 11 that falls inside water or damaged by Water

If catastrophe has struck your iPad Pro 11, do not worry. Even if you immerse your iPad Pro 11 into a full tub of water; all hope is probably not lost. It is normal to presume water splashing on an iPad Pro 11 leading to electric shock, dark smoke, and damaged screen. Nonetheless, it can be harder than you think for water to reach that circuitry. Also, one of the top motives for iPad Pro 11 failing after being submerged in water is the electric battery turning out to be corroded, which will not occur immediately.

You will find two exceptional types of water hazard as it pertains to an iPad Pro 11; therefore, there are two specific actions you have to take. The first problem is when spilling water on an iPad Pro 11. This has similar hazards combined with the iPad Pro 11 being unintentionally sprayed with water. The next form of risk is the iPad Pro 11 being dipped or immersed into plenty of water in a shower, a pool, a lake, and many more.

How to proceed if you spilled water on your iPad Pro 11

This is where you honestly desire you have an incredible accessory shielding your device. Trust it or not, the iPad Pro 11 is remarkably waterproof. The exterior part of the iPad Pro 11 is dominated by an aluminium framework, which gives water little chance to get into the iPad Pro 11. Even the rims are improbable to permit any water through from the time water is spilt on the iPad Pro 11 to when you clean it clean.

This leaves a few parts of the device to save from problems such as the speakers, the headphone jack, the lightning connector, the volume buttons, the power button, and the home button.

When you have your iPad Pro 11 wrapped in a smart case or an identical cushty-healthy case, it is impossible for water to get into it. You need to carefully dry the iPad Pro 11, noting whether or no more any water become pooled across the home button, and then cautiously take away the case and then wiping away any water, inspect the rims of the iPad Pro 11 for any water, paying the most interest to the inside of the iPad Pro 11.

If the surface is dry and there's no water on the home button, you're likely fine. However, it's usually best to leave the iPad Pro 11 unused for about 24 to 48 hours only to be sure it's fine.

I've experienced an iPad Pro 11 survived the spillage of a

full glass of water directly on the screen. It is significant how accurate the experience of the smart case can maintain times of non-permanent clumsiness.

If you weren't lucky to have your iPad Pro 11 protected during such incidence, you might have to adhere to the instructions for handling a completely submerged iPad Pro 11. If you just got some water on the screen, so you realize it didn't get close to the control keys, especially the home button, or the sound system/loudspeaker or USB slot, you would be right wiping it down. However, if water went everywhere into the iPad Pro 11, play it secure by assuming water made its way into the panel.

How to Fix iPad Pro 11 Submerged in Liquid or water

You might have noticed how an iPad Pro 11 or iPad Pro 11 or a few other devices can be fixed after been plunged into a box of rice and remains there for a day. The main advantage of this process, sagely advice time would help save a damp iPad Pro 11.

Research by Gazelle relates how rice, oatmeal, and even silica gel packets may not be almost as absorbent as we might think. Moreover, a silica gel packet won't suck water through Aluminium.

If you have noticed how some crystallized types of kitty litter are much like silica gel, remember they're additionally no more than rice (or smaller!).

If you wish to be more secure, use silica gel packets.

They will not get caught of one's iPad Pro 11 and cause more problems.

After absolutely drying the outer area of the iPad Pro 11 with a very soft towel or fabric; the huge decision is if to turn ON or OFF the iPad Pro 11. If the iPad Pro 11 continued to be ON and powered, this choice is more straightforward: switch it OFF by pressing down the Power button and then either sliding the button to power it OFF when brought ON or to press down the Power button before iPad Pro 11 shut down itself.

Recall, the iPad Pro 11 being in sleep mode isn't like the iPad Pro 11 being shut down. The different parts of the iPad Pro 11 are nonetheless running at precisely the same time as it is in sleep mode, and most severe, the iPad Pro 11 can awaken itself if you have a notification, text, Facetime call, etc.

However, if the iPad Pro 11 has already been in sleep mode, waking it up to shut it down may be worse than leaving it in droop/sleep mode. This depends on one main thing: the chance that something will be needed to awaken the display. This can be a scheduled appointment reminder; a smartphone call routed to the iPad Pro 11, a message, a Facebook notification, etc. It would help if you chose to turn off the iPad Pro 11 to allow it dried out.

If possible, move the cursor around in progress and wake the iPad Pro 11 up and immediately shut it down with the use of the Power button and the instructions mentioned above. In many cases, the probability of the iPad Pro 11 getting up may be impossible; in cases like this removing it from sleep mode is excellent.

Do's and Don'ts

- **Don't:** use a locks dryer or leave your iPad Pro 11 near a heater or use any form of warmness which you wouldn't usually blast on your arm for one hour. A higher amount of heat can damage an iPad Pro 11.

- **Do:** Leave your iPad Pro 11 for at the least a day and ideally 48 hours. You will need to leave the iPad Pro 11 seated up with the home button at the lowest (bottom level). Gravity is your friend. If any water made it into the iPad Pro 11, it likely managed to get in through the home button, lightning interface, or bottom loudspeakers. Leaving your iPad Pro 11 position up for two times can help that dampness make its way from the iPad Pro 11. When you have an iPad Pro 11 with four audio speakers like the iPad Pro 11 Pro, you could wait a day and then turn the iPad Pro 11 position for the next day. This may optimistically permit any water to drip out through the sound system (loudspeakers).

If you want to use silica gel packets, be sure the iPad Pro 11 is in the upright position. Gravity remains your best friend, so you should make sure it's working for you as well as the gel packets.

My iPad Pro 11 cannot Power ON after being left for hours

With a little luck, the mere truth that the iPad Pro 11 sat for a few days is enough for just any stray wetness in the iPad Pro 11 to evaporate. If the iPad Pro 11 does not **Power ON** or if it'll power on but has apparent problems with changing colours on the screen or it freezes immediately, you must take it to the nearest Apple Store or dispatch it to Apple. A common cause for water damage and mould to intervene with an iPad Pro 11 is the harm done to the battery, and a battery may be all you have to get it working once again.

You can discover an apple retail region by using this web page https://www.apple.com/retail you may even reach apple's tech support team at +1-800-676-2775.

CPSIA information can be obtained
at www.ICGtesting.com
Printed in the USA
LVHW051058170321
681672LV00022B/1564